A Brief and Exact Account

The Recollections of Simão Rodrigues
on the Origin and Progress of the Society of Jesus

A Brief and Exact Account

The Recollections of Simão Rodrigues
on the Origin and Progress of the Society of Jesus

With Translation, Introduction, and Commentary by
Joseph F. Conwell, S.J.

Saint Louis
The Institute of Jesuit Sources

To all Jesuits, past, present, and to come,

imperfect, one and all,

yet bound in fidelity to their Lord.

No. 20 in Series I: Jesuit Primary
Sources in English Translations

Library of Congress Control Number 2004112733
ISBN 1-880810-56-5

CONTENTS

INTRODUCTION

Toward the end of his life, Simão Rodrigues, one of the first companions of St. Ignatius in Paris, was asked by the fourth General of the Society of Jesus, Everard Mercurian, to give an account of the origins of the Society. Responding in Latin from Lisbon on 25 July 1577,[1] the author is somewhat distrustful of "an old man's memory" [1] and does not want to leave out anything of importance. In 1577 he is sixty-seven years old and will die two years later. With an old man's memory for the details of his youth, he fills in more of the background outlined briefly by another of the original companions, Diego Laínez, in a letter written 30 years earlier to Juan de Polanco, the Secretary of the Society, in response to his request for information about the nascent Society.[2] He does, indeed, make a few errors of fact, but by and large his narrative is trustworthy.

In the *Monumenta* edition the Latin text is accompanied by another text in Portuguese which is not a translation of the Latin original. Whether it was written before or after the Latin is not clear; it may, rather, represent the first draft of the document. It does, however, seem to have been written in the sixteenth rather than the seventeenth century. See *FN* 3:5-7.

Although this translation is basically from the Latin, on occasion the Portuguese has been helpful in clarifying the meaning of the passage and I have not blushed to dip into the Portuguese without cluttering the text with footnotes to that effect.

Some notes are added to this document, frequently drawn from comments by the editors of the *Monumenta* edition. They are meant to clarify persons, places, events, and times. The references to Schurhammer's life of Francis Xavier in German have been changed to refer to Georg Schurhammer, S.J., *Francis Xavier: His Life, His Times,*

---

[1] *Commentarium de origine et progressu Societatis Iesu,* MHSI 85:8-135 (Latin and Portuguese).

[2] 16 June 1547, *Monumenta Historica Societatis Iesu* [MHSI] 66: *Fontes Narrativi* [FN] 1:70-145 [L] [Spanish and Latin].

Vol. 1: Europe (1506-1541), tr. M. Joseph Costelloe, S.J. (Rome: The Jesuit Historical Institute, 1973), abbreviated to *GS.*

Special attention needs to be given by a competent scholar to the author, Simão Rodrigues. Garcia Villoslada, a Jesuit who has written a new biography of Ignatius in Spanish, considers Simão obsessed with sex. Maybe so. He seems to have been a very attractive person, especially as a young man. "Everyone" in Portugal fell in love with him. He also appears to have been something of an athlete, although fasting and other rigors weakened his health considerably. He also seems to have been somewhat naive, an innocent wandering around in a world inclined to evil. He may also have been a skilled rhetorician, and there may be much more in the text than meets the eye. Someone needs to do a rhetorical analysis of the text after the fashion of Marjorie O'Rourke Boyle, who approached the *Autobiography* of Ignatius from a rhetorical point of view and has shed much light on that text.[3] She has done similar studies on Erasmus and others.[4] Rodrigues, for example, is prone to make scriptural allusions without indicating that he is doing so. Many are pointed out here, but many more probably lie hidden in the text.

In the telling, Simão is much influenced by the *Spiritual Exercises* and, it would seem, the literary form of the medieval romance, very popular in his day, in which valiant knights like Roland, Galahad, and Amadis of Gaul, real, mythical, or fictional, fight giants and dragons and monsters of every kind, endure dangers and labors on land and sea, rescue those in distress, assist the poor and the weak, all for the honor and glory of their lord or their lady.

Recall that Ignatius, before his conversion, was enamored of chivalry. His ancestors had fought at Beotíbar in 1321, the battle that thereafter bound his family in fealty to the King of Castille. Beltran, the father of Ignatius, fought for their Catholic Majesties, Ferdinand and Isabella, during the Grenada crusade. Ignatius's eldest brother,

---

[3] Marjorie O'Rourke Boyle, *Loyola's Acts: The Rhetoric of the Self* (Berkeley: University of California Press, 1997.

[4] *Erasmus on Language and Method in Theology* (Toronto: University of Toronto Press, 1977); *Rhetoric and Reform: Erasmus's Civil Dispute with Luther* (Cambridge: Harvard Historical Monographs LXXI, 1983); *Petrarch's Genius: Pentimento and Prophecy* (Berkeley: University of California Press, 1991).

Juan, along with another brother named Beltran, died in the Naples campaign of 1498. Another brother, Hernando, went to the Indies seeking conquest, and died in South America. Martín, heir to Loyola after the death of Juan, fought against the French. Iñigo not only rallied the troops at Pamplona, but in his convalescence daydreamed about the great feats of arms he would perform in the service of a high-born lady. In his conversion the lady of his dreams was transformed into the Virgin Mother of God, and the lord whom he swore to serve with eternal fealty was no longer a temporal prince but the King of Kings, Christ the Lord. He abandoned completely the medieval knight's pursuit of honor as his highest value, and sought instead the greater honor and glory of God. This chivalric frame of mind he shared with his followers, and this fact should be kept in mind during the reading of Rodrigues's account.

Perhaps Simão is influenced by his experience of medieval mystery plays (mystery here meaning God's mysterious way of acting in human history), but if so, then this letter covers only a small part of a gigantic passion play being enacted across the centuries by an ever-changing cast of players.

Rodrigues begins by introducing the cast of characters in his mystery play about a benevolent lord and his vassals, if that is indeed what he intends it to be. The first is God, the Lord Most High, Creator of the Society of Jesus out of nothing but weak and faulty human beings, just as he had created the human race out of the slime of the earth. "God, the Lord Most High, watched over our Society right from the very beginning by starting it and drawing it closely together," [1] just as God first created and then adorned the earth. The companions used the same language in the document summarizing the account of their election to request that the pope recognize the Society as a body within the Church, "Since the most merciful and gracious Lord had deigned to unite us to one another and to gather us together. . .we should not sever the bonding and the gathering."[5] From tiny beginnings the power of God brought the Society of Jesus to a certain fullness and grandeur, just as he always brings marvelous wonders out of nothing. In the days of chivalry, a good and benevolent lord was as bound in fidelity to his vassals as his vassals were bound in fidelity to

---

[5] "The Deliberation of the First Fathers," *Const.* 1:17 [3].

him. The story, then, is about how God chose them, called them, united them, inspired them, tested them, and confirmed their election. From the beginning, God is the main actor.

After introducing God, Simão introduces the group of players in whom God will work divine marvels, for the plot of the story is how God deals with the group. God had acted in each one during the Spiritual Exercises, moving each to make the independent election to go to the Holy Land. Becoming aware of their unanimity, they freely elected to go to Jerusalem together as a group, and further elected that if they found no passage within a year, they would offer themselves as a group to the pope to go wherever he wished. The story, then, is about how God confirmed their election. Note that from the beginning Rodrigues sets out to tell the story, not of what Ignatius and his companions did in founding the Society and getting it moving, but the story of how God worked in them in doing what they did. This story is part of God's story—another fact should be kept in mind in interpreting each and every paragraph.

In the *Spiritual Exercises* the consideration on the Call of the King (*SpEx* 91-98), the consideration on the Two Standards (*SpEx* 149-57) and the explanation of the Three Ways of Being Humble (*SpEx* 165-68) are filled with the spirit of medieval chivalry. The imaginary king chosen by God says, "Come with me, share my food and drink and clothing; labor with me, watch with me, share in my victory as you share in my toil." One not answering the call would be considered an unworthy knight. Jesus, the eternal King, also says, "Come with me, labor with me; follow me in pain, and follow me in glory." The deserved response is wholehearted devotion, or even better, a passionate desire to serve the Lord by offering to imitate Jesus in bearing injuries and affronts, actual poverty and spiritual poverty if it is for his greater service and praise. In the Two Standards the false promises and deceits of Satan are laid bare, the snares and chains in riches and honors. Jesus invites to poverty and humiliation if they serve his Father better, to deepest humility in order to be like him. In the vision at La Storta, not far from Rome, Ignatius experienced himself placed by the Father at the side of Christ carrying his cross, and he heard the words, "I will be propitious to you [vobis = plural]." In Rome Ignatius told his companions that they would have to suffer many contradictions there (*Autobiography* 96-97).

Simão was so taken by the Three Ways of Being Humble (*SpEx* 165-68) that when he eventually became the provincial in Portugal, he schooled the scholastics in Coimbra especially in practicing ways of choosing "poverty with Christ poor rather than wealth, contempt with Christ laden with it rather than honors." The scholastics went to excess, and Simão appealed to Ignatius to bring about some sort of balance. In his response to Fr. General Mercurian, it is clear that Simão had been profoundly impressed by the way his companions from the beginning freely embraced sharing Christ's poverty and humiliation.

Nothing marks the valiant knight so clearly as his utter and complete devotion to the lord to whose service he has committed himself. He will follow his lord wherever he goes, whatever hardships he endures. He wishes to share whatever happens to his lord. Likewise, there are no "grays" in Simão's telling; all is black or white, or in vivid, living color. God is all powerful and works in weakness; the evil spirit is the master of darkness and confusion. The companions are like the knights of old, brilliant, performing mighty deeds in their weakness and lowliness through the power of God, overcoming all obstacles, and holy in their poverty, which is extreme. They struggle with heretics, with the weather, with the terrain; they serve the poor, the sick, the dying. Sin abounds, but grace abounds still more. The colors are dazzling, the actions intense; the ordinary humdrum of daily life has been banished. They live to the full the ideals of chivalry.

Simão Rodrigues tells the story of God at work in the Society as though it is a continuation of the *Acts of the Apostles*. Like *Acts* this is a travel story. We find the same incredible successes, the same confrontations with the opposition, the casting out of devils, the conversion of sinners, the vilification of the good, sinful women and holy women, trials before various authorities, marvelous acts of divine providence, difficulties by land and by water, ending up in Rome, accomplishing much good, and waiting.

During that time, the Society had increased from 10 members to 5000. In the process of telling, after the manner of *Acts*, what God had done with the companions during their trip from Paris to Venice to Loreto to Rome and back to Venice and again to Rome, ending with the founding of the Society of Jesus through Pope Paul III's confirmation of the Institute, Rodrigues not only reveals to those five thousand

members[6] the spirit that impelled the first companions, but manages
to achieve a number of different goals.[7]

First of all, by telling the story of God's acting in the companions,
transforming their election to go to the Holy Land into the deliberate
choice of founding the Society of Jesus, he illustrates the main ele-
ments of the Formula: the central place of mission in the new Society,
the nature and scope of that mission, and the works the Society per-
forms in order to accomplish the mission. Regarding mission, he illustrates the primacy for mission of a commitment to God in celibate
chastity, the fundamental interior disposition for mission of poverty,
the basic dictate for mission of obedience to Christ in his vicar, the
pope, and the imperative for mission of obedience to Christ recognized in one of the companions. Regarding the end and scope of the
Society, he illustrates the longing of the companions to share their gift
of faith with those who are not Christians (here called infidels), their
eagerness to bring other Christians (here called heretics) back to the
primitive unity of Catholic Christianity, and their zeal in enabling
Catholics to grow in their faith. The works he describes are the ministry of the Word: preaching, lecturing, and other forms of ministry of
the Word, like exhortations and private conversations; giving the
Spiritual Exercises; teaching Christian doctrine to children and those
not versed in the Christian faith; hearing confessions and administering the other sacraments; reconciling those who are estranged
from one another; serving those in hospitals; taking care of the poor.
He does not mention visiting those in prison, but he does indicate that

---

[6] Did Mercurian communicate Simão's story to the rest of the Society? The original
Latin version sent to Mercurian rests in the Society's archives in Rome. The Portuguese
version is in the Biblioteca nacional in Lisbon. A Spanish version is also housed in the
Biblioteca nacional in Lisbon, and the Society's archives in Rome has a brief compendi-
um made in the 18th century. There is no evidence, therefore, that Fr. Mercurian
ordered that the letter be copied and be disseminated widely throughout the Society.
There is evidence that Ribadeneira knew of the letter, but no evidence that he saw it,
quite the contrary. The letter was known, certainly, by Nicholas Orlandini (1554-1606)
and Francis Sacchini (1570-1625), two of the Society's earliest historians, who not only
praised it highly but drew on it in minute detail. What a loss if the General did not dis-
seminate the document!

[7] The first Formula proposed by the companions was approved orally by Paul III
in 1539. A slightly modified form was solemnly approved in writing in 1540.
Experience dictated some improvements in 1550 under Julius III; Rodrigues has in
mind the 1550 version. Since then the Formula has remained unchanged. Here we follow the content of the 1550 version.

the companions themselves are threatened with imprisonment. Everywhere the companions go, they go in poverty, they care for the poor, and they care for the sick, carrying out the mission of Jesus, who preached the Word, healed the sick, and showed special concern for the marginalized.

Secondly, in this letter Rodrigues illustrates the main points of the Spiritual Exercises: the overcoming of self, the need for balance or readiness otherwise known as indifference, the rejection of sin and worldly ambitions and attachments, commitment to Jesus, the efforts of the evil spirit to weaken commitment through temptations and trials, fearless following in the footsteps of Jesus, openness to poverty and humiliation, suffering for the sake of Jesus, joy in discovering him along the way, deliberately electing to maintain the union God had given them by offering themselves as a body to the pope to go wherever he might send them, rising with Jesus above all human limitations and expectations, finding him at work in the darkest and dreariest moments, experiencing his presence when he seems most far away. "Let not your hearts be troubled," when things seem to be turned inside out and upside down: peace is not the work of the world but of the Holy Spirit who sends down fire to make all things new.

Thirdly, in this letter Rodrigues illustrates sharply and clearly that God works his mighty deeds with and in and through faulty human instruments. Sometimes the author names them. Sometimes "one of the Fathers" (usually Simão himself) is the faulty instrument. Once God has formed the group, what happens to one happens to all; the experience of one stands for the experiences of each. For the most part, therefore, there is no need for Simão to identify individual members by name. They depart from Paris filled with joy. But the first night out one of them, probably Rodrigues, discovers a bloody blister caused by his shoulder strap. Simão describes the turmoil suffered in the darkness of the night, the horror, the fear, the haunting question whether he can continue the journey, the dark demons of doubt that overwhelm him. A blister! The morning light reveals no sign of a blister. What a vivid and striking symbol of desolation: painful, petty, deserving little attention, annoying, distracting, enervating, changing the focus from God to self, followed by a return to consolation: everyone's experience. It is also a metaphor of God's fidelity to those he has chosen to serve him.

In this story of God at work we should not expect human perfection but imperfection. For example:

(1) the 16th century was not noted for the ability of some of its greatest men to listen to one another quietly and calmly in an attempt to learn from one another. The companions soon learned that their approach to what Vatican II would call "our separated brethren" was not fruitful. In a letter that one of the companions, Peter Faber, wrote a few years later to another companion, Diego Laínez, he says that we should first of all love them, then fight against any negative thoughts or feelings about them, bring them to love us, speak about our agreements rather than our disagreements, urge them to growth in prayer and virtue, in morality and the love of God.[8]

(2) The attitude of the companions toward women is far from perfect, but it is not likely that in their time and culture they would have understood many of the concerns of Decree 14 of the 34th General Congregation of the Society of Jesus (1995) regarding "Jesuits and the Situation of Women in Church and Civil Society."[9] Misogynism in any form or at any time is worthy of condemnation since it does great harm to women especially but also to men, but even so some attempt should be made to understand the misogynist.

(3) The companions were certainly more credulous than most Jesuits would be in similar situations today, but they were profoundly aware of God present and acting in their lives and aware also of the presence of evil with which they were in conflict.

One final characteristic of Simão Rodrigues's writing style should be noted. Since the story is about events that took place in the past, he normally employs the past tense (in Latin, either the perfect tense or the imperfect tense). In his enthusiasm, however, in the middle of a sentence he often changes to the present tense as though the action is taking place at that very moment. In order to preserve that sense of enthusiasm, the present translation often accepts and follows that change, even at the risk of annoying some readers.

---

[8] 7 March 1546; MF 399-402.
[9] *Documents of the Thirty-Fourth General Congregation of the Society of Jesus* (The Institute of Jesuit Sources, Saint Louis, 1995), 171-178.

Editor's Note Regarding Abbreviations in Footnotes

1. Two abbreviations are found repeatedly in the footnotes of all seven chapters of this book. They are:

a. *FN*: This means "Fontes Narrativi," and refers in general to the multi-volume series *Monumenta Historica Societatis Iesu,* and ordinarily to volume 85 in that series (*Fontes Narrativi de Sancto Ignatio de Loyola et de Societatis Iesu Initiis,* ed. Candido de Dalmases, S.I. [Rome: 1960]), especially pages 8-135.

b. *GS*: Georg Schurhammer, S.I., *Francis Xavier: His Life and Times, Vol. 1: Europe, 1506-1541,* tr. M. Joseph Costelloe, S.I., (Rome: Jesuit Historical Institute, 1973).

2. Other abbreviations occur only rarely.

a. for the most part these refer to one or other of the volumes of the *Monumenta Historica,* already referred to. In alphabetical order, these are:

EB = *Epistolae Broët* (Letters of Paschase Broët, Claude Jay, John Codure, and Simão Rodrigues) or *Epistolae Bobadillae* (Letters of Nicholás Bobadilla)

EI = *Epistolae Ignatii* (Letters of St. Ignatius)

EL = *Epistolae Laínez* (Letters of James Lainez)

EM = *Epistolae Mixtae* (Letters from various sources)

EX = *Epistolae Xavier* (Letters of St. Francis Xavier)

FD = *Fontes Documentales de Sancto Ignatio* (vol. 115 of *Monumenta;* material dealing with Ignatius's family, fatherland, youth, and first companions)

MF = *Monumenta Fabri* (Letters, etc., of Peter Faber).

b. Other abbreviations used occasionally by the author include:

C = *Constitutiones Societatis Iesu* (Constitutions of the Society)

ET = English translation

L = Latin text

[L plus an Arabic number (e.g., [L33])] = Laínez's letter to Polanco of 1547: *FN* 1:70-145

OED = Oxford English Dictionary

TV = Pietro Tacchi-Venturi, *Storia della Compagnia di Gesu in Italia* (1910).

CHAPTER ONE: The People Involved

TO THE VERY REVEREND IN CHRIST FATHER EVERARD MERCURIAN, GENERAL OF THE SOCIETY OF JESUS:

A SHORT NARRATIVE OF THE ORIGINS AND PROGRESS OF THE SAME SOCIETY UP TO ITS CONFIRMATION

Very Reverend Father in Christ,

[1] Over and over again many persons in different places have asked me to write down an exact account of how our gracious and powerful God watched over our Society right from the very beginning by starting it and drawing it closely together, and I have refused. I have even been reluctant to write anything down after giving a brief account of events I had not forgotten to those who asked about them. These stories I shall now write down in joyful obedience to Your Paternity's command. I am afraid, however, that an old man like myself might leave out many details, since the memory of old people is usually less reliable, and the events I am about to write happened forty years ago.[1]

> *Commentary:* The opening lines are deceptively simple. The reader might find it helpful to compare and contrast the salutation with Luke's opening lines to Theophilus in the Acts of the Apostles, and compare and contrast the first paragraph with the opening paragraph of Luke's Gospel. Fr. General is Simão's Theophilus (whose very name means "Beloved of God," an indication of what "Your Paternity" means to Simão). Whereas in Acts Luke stated that in the Gospel he wrote about what Jesus did and taught, Simão does not set out to narrate what Ignatius and his companions did, but what God (that is to say, Jesus) did in them. Ignatius and his companions were convinced that Jesus was the head of their company, that Jesus founded the Society. The story Simão tells is not their story, but God's story. Simão's intent is to continue the story that Luke began. Luke told how Jesus forged a bond with his disciples

[1] Rodrigues begins his narrative with the vows of the companions at Montmarte in 1534. Hence, 43 years had elapsed before he began or at least finished this letter.

1

that continues in the Church today, and Simão is about to tell the story of how God (Jesus) started the Society and created in it a similar bond of
unity. Keeping in mind that Simão is narrating God's story, how God worked in, through, and with Ignatius and his companions, the reader will understand and interpret each paragraph more easily. In Luke's Gospel many others had attempted to narrate Jesus' story; according to Simão's letter many had asked him to write the story of the Society, but he refused to do so until Fr. General asked, the one who for Simão held the place of Jesus. In Acts 2:12 the crowd on Pentecost heard the apostles "speaking about God's deeds of power [*magnalia Dei*]." In Acts 14:27, after making a long tour through Asia Minor, Paul and Barnabas called the Church in Antioch together "and related all that God had done with them."

First of all I shall say this to Your Reverend Paternity. I have often reflected on how the power of God alone raised the Society from small beginnings to its present grandeur, and I have recalled and mulled over how the same God and author of all things made our first parent Adam the source and head of the whole human race out of the slime of the earth; and also that by his wonderful counsel the same God first made this whole beautiful universe out of nothing, then adorned it, and brought order into it as the days and months and years passed. And so it seems to me that this must be said about the beginning of the Society: The Lord has done this [Ps. 118:23] and as it pleased the Lord, so it was done [Job 1:21]. Lest anyone be ignorant of his infinite power, whatever he has cultivated, he has made from nothing, and out of little things he alone makes great wonders [Ps. 136:4]. Therefore we all owe him honor and praise as the all-powerful source and author of the Society for the great things he has done in it and will do in the future.

> *Commentary:* Luke 5 tells the story of how Jesus converted Peter's all-night "non-catch" of fish into a wondrously abundant harvest. The Society is another instance of how "God chose what is foolish in the world to shame the wise . . . what is weak . . . to shame the strong . . . what is low and despised . . , things that are not, to reduce to nothing things that are, so that no one might boast in the presence of God" (2 Cor. 1:27-29).

[2] To finish our task more quickly, let us get to the matter at hand.

All of us who belong to the Society know that God delineated its first form and shape at the University of Paris of high renown, at the time that the deadly infection of Luther's heresy, hidden though it was, began to invade Paris and other flourishing cities in France. God, who is wonderfully provident and faithful, countered this evil like a wise and compassionate father of a family who brings out from his storehouse both new things and old (Mt. 13:52) as they are needed. When poisonous thorns sprouted afresh in the Church's field, God chose to employ new workers. With singular kindness God bestowed upon the world the Society of Jesus, at once ancient and utterly new, so that the sons of this Society, like Ruth the faithful Moabitess, in the spirit of humble solicitude might follow in the footsteps of earlier harvesters and gather from the harvest field of the Lord the ears of grain that escaped their hands (Ruth 2:2-3).

> *Commentary:* Jerome Nadal, whom Ignatius chose to promulgate the Constitutions of the Society of Jesus, also used the image of Ruth to describe the role of the Society in the Church: "Wherefore it is necessary for Ours especially to reverence and praise religious orders, holding ourselves to be the lowliest, unworthy to be religious, and in accordance with the grace of our vocation holding other religious in high regard as they deserve. We should rather regard ourselves as another Ruth who followed after the reapers, gathering the ears they let fall as they carried forward great bundles of grain. Therefore we ought to consider it a particular grace that Our Lord has given to his Church in sending this Company along at the rear, and the Society should consider it a particular grace that is commonly not merited. If the Lord does not call someone, exhortations and admonitions and exercises are of no avail: 'You did not choose me, but I have chosen you.'" (*MN* 5:262, alternate reading, lines 71-76, Exhortation 3[a] in Alcalá.) In 1995 the 34th General Congregation put the same idea in this way: "The focus of Christ's mission is the prophetic proclamation of the Gospel that challenges people in the name of the Kingdom of his Father; we are to preach that Kingdom in poverty. He calls us to be at the very heart of the world's experience as it receives this promise of the Kingdom and is brought to receive God's gift in its fullness. . . . He calls us 'to help men and women disengage themselves from the tarnished and confused image that

they have in themselves in order to discover that they are, in God's light, completely like Christ.[2] And so we undertake our ministries with a confidence that the Lord takes us, as He did Ignatius, as his servants—not because we are strong, but because he says to us, as he said to St. Paul, 'My grace is sufficient for you, for my power is made perfect in weakness (2 Cor. 12:9).'" (GC34, Decree 2, n. 6, *Servants of Christ's Mission*.)

[3] Besides, all of us in the Society are aware how God our Lord in his abundant goodness and mercy chose ten men in those early days to be the first foundation of this magnificent edifice. Some were Spaniards, some French, trained in theology at the University of Paris. The first of these was that blessed Father[3] of happy memory, Master Ignatius, a Spaniard from that part of Cantabria that is commonly called Guipúzcoa, born of the illustrious family of Loyola. After renouncing the illusions of this vale of tears and dedicating himself completely to the divine service, he burned incessantly with an intense desire for the salvation of the human race. Divine Wisdom (who chose him from his mother's womb to be the cornerstone of this new building) also tested him through many difficult trials in which he remained faithful to the end. Indeed, it is by hammering and pushing that polished stones are fitted into place by the hand of the craftsman. The others always revered him as their father and followed him as their leader in carrying out many difficult tasks and in attempting many others. Eventually, some years later, they unanimously chose him as the General of the Society of Jesus.

> *Commentary:* Ignatius was born Iñigo de Loyola, probably in 1491, the youngest of thirteen brothers and sisters. Basque was his native language, Spanish clearly a second language. Rodrigues sees Ignatius as part of that line of great men in the Old and New Testaments whom God chose from the womb for a special role in salvation history. Ignatius is the cornerstone of the Society just as Jesus is the cornerstone of the Church in Acts 4:11. Simão's Latin text abbreviates and reflects a verse from the hymn in the old Latin breviary at First Vespers for the Dedication of a Church which, translated into English, reads:

[2] Peter-Hans Kolvenbach, Discourse to General Congregation 34, 6 January 1995; cf. Appendix II, pt. 2, of *Documents of the Thirty-Fourth General Congregation of the Society of Jesus*, St. Louis: Institute of Jesuit Sources, 1995), p. 266.

[3] Rodrigues calls each of the Paris companions "Father" even though none was ordained when they first gathered in Paris.

By many a weary blow that broke / Or polished with a work-
man's skill, / The stones. . . all are fitly framed to lie / In their
appointed place on high."[4]

[4] The second was Master Peter Faber, a Savoyard. Moved by a warm,
holy relationship with Father Ignatius, and out of admiration for his
life, he made a notable change in his way of life and consecrated himself with his whole heart to God. He began to be inflamed with an
incredible desire to go to Jerusalem and the holy places, and to spend
his life for the salvation of human beings. He longed to call them out
of darkness[5] into the light of truth and from death to life. This Father,
if I may omit his many other virtues, was especially endowed with
charming grace in dealing with people, which up to now I must con-
fess I have not seen in anyone else. Somehow he entered into friend-
ships in such a way, bit by bit coming to influence others in such a
manner, that his very way of living and his gracious conversation
powerfully drew to the love of God all those with whom he dealt.

> *Commentary:* Peter Faber was born in 1506 in an Alpine village
> belonging to the Duchy of Savoy. As a boy he look care of the
> sheep. Having exhausted the local educational possibilities, he
> had gone to Paris to finish his studies. The description of Peter
> Faber recalls the testimony of St. Paul to Agrippa that God has
> sent him to the Gentiles "to open their eyes so that they may
> turn from darkness to light and from the power of Satan to
> God" (Acts 26:18). The companions carry on the work begun in
> Acts.

[5] The third was Master Francis Xavier, a Navarrese. At the time
these events took place he was with the two Fathers mentioned above.
They were all studying at the College of St. Barbara, living in different
rooms in the same house. Influenced by their actions and by living
together with them, Xavier abandoned his old way of life. Adopting a

---

[4] E.T. from *The Roman Breviary* (New York: Benziger Brothers, 1964, 130b.
[5] Cf. also 1 Pt. 2:9 ". . . who called you out of darkness into his own marvelous
light."

better one, he gives himself completely to the salvation of others and a pilgrimage to the holy places of Jerusalem.[6] He was always strong and constant in anything he undertook: although on fire with burning zeal, he subdued and overcame himself so that he was able to teach Aristotelian philosophy for three and a half years in the College, if I remember correctly, of Beauvais.[7] After carrying out this task in an outstanding manner, he withdrew to some secret place to give himself assiduously to prayer, penance, and communion with Christ, communicating frequently with Father Ignatius, rarely with the other companions.[8] In the matter of corporal penances he was sometimes well intentioned but imprudent in his fervor: he bound the muscles of his arms and hips so tightly with ropes and interlaced them in such a way that they swelled so that the ropes were scarcely visible. The swelling was so great that there was no hope of cutting the ropes.[9] Meanwhile in great distress the other companions kept praying for him. He was terribly afflicted by this grave condition for about two days, and the companions were afraid that one of his arms which was more tightly bound might have to be cut off, when he recovered completely by the singular mercy of God (while I did not grasp at all the reason for this sudden recovery) so that many human beings, both Christians and those with no faith in Christ, might attain eternal happiness through his industrious work. Let great thanks therefore be given to God the author of all goodness.

> *Commentary:* Francis Xavier was born of a noble family 7 April 1506, six days before Peter Faber. Each of the companions made the Spiritual Exercises under the direction of Ignatius or of Peter

[6] Xavier's conversion took place between December 1532 and June 1533. *GS* 187[262], *FN* 3:12[10].

[7] After completing his philosophical studies Xavier became a regent, teaching in the College of Dormans-Beauvais from October 1, 1530 until the summer of 1534. The college is not far from the College of St. Barbara on the street named after Jean Beauvais. It gets its name from Jean de Dormans, bishop of Beauvais, a cardinal who founded the college in 1370. *GS* 148-49, *FN* 3:12[11].

[8] Xavier made the Spiritual Exercises in September 1534, after the vows at Montmartre on August 15. He had not been able to make them earlier because his teaching duties interfered. Cf. Luís Gonçalves da Câmara, *Memoriale*, n. 138, *FN* 1:610; *GS* 216, *FN* 3:13[12].

[9] Da Câmara indicates that Xavier was one of the best jumpers in the university and suggests that he was trying to mortify his passion for jumping. *Memoriale FN* 1:705, n. 306. See *FN* 3:14[13].

Faber after Ignatius left Paris. Simão here refers to September 1534 when Francis Xavier was making the Exercises after already determining to pilgrimage to the Holy Land with the other companions. The Exercises have as their purpose "to overcome oneself and to order one's life, without reaching a decision through some disordered affection" (*SpEx* 21). In telling the story of Xavier, Simão is illustrating the dangers inherent in inordinate attachments and the necessity of being free of them in order to be able to choose what "is more conducive to the end for which I am created," as stated in the "First Principle and Foundation" (*SpEx* 23). The seductive attraction to excessive penance was in the beginning too much for Xavier, as it had been for Ignatius, and would be for many Jesuits like St. Francis Borgia and Antony Araoz, the first provincial of Spain.

[6] Since we have said that this Father withdrew to a secret place so that he might give himself more fully to prayer, it will not be out of place to insert here what happened to another Father[10] in a similar situation. This other Father had a room in the home of a private citizen and was preparing to expiate for his sins by a general confession, as is customary in the Society. Immediately after dinner a servant girl approaches him first of all with honeyed words and lewd gestures, and then, entwining him in her arms, tries to drag him to the ground in order to commit the shameful crime she has in mind. The Father resists and shoves her away even as she fights back. Finally repulsed, she weeps bitterly and in shame leaves the man, crying out as she leaves, "You are really gross, a savage beast." By the grace of God this Father was victorious in this encounter and in others no less dangerous.

Commentary: Here Simão tells of his own making of the Spiritual Exercises, and speaks of the attraction to sex which can divert a man's attention from a call from God. Perhaps he has in mind the prostitute in Prov. 7:21: "With much seductive speech she persuades him; with her smooth talk she compels him." Like the story of the temptation in the Garden of Eden, it is set in the context of eating, and just as the seductive serpent winds itself around the tree in many a depiction of the garden story, so the

[10]This unnamed companion seems to be Simão Rodrigues, and so, in general, throughout the narrative.

seductive woman winds herself around Simão. The woman in
this story is very unlike the sinful woman in Luke 7:36-49 who
threw herself at the feet of Jesus and bathed his feet with her
tears. Simão is illustrating one point of the First Week of the
Exercises by suggesting how destructive sin could be to the one
who yields to its enticements. By joining his story of the
woman's arms around his neck with that of Xavier and the
ropes around his arms, Simão seems to be reminding us of the
story of Samson and Delilah; Samson is bound first by the sexual blandishments of a woman and then by heavy cords, but the
grace and power of God prevail. Simão is expressing the conviction of the companions that they are caught up in the stream
of salvation history running through both the Old and New
Testaments.

[7] A Portugese holds the fourth spot,[11] who because of his unworthi-
ness does not merit to have his name mentioned along with these
other outstanding and perfect servants of God. Of him I shall make
this one remark so as not to interrupt the narrative, that he was a man
divinely impelled, wondrously aroused by God to change his former
way of life to one of divine service. I will note besides that he had
never before had anything to do with Father Ignatius, but only hearing of his great sanctity he decided to lay open to him all his thoughts
and feelings; unaware of what the other three had in mind he decided
to go to Jerusalem and to spend his whole life in working for the salvation of his neighbor.

> *Commentary:* Simão Rodrigues was born about 1510 in Vouzela,
> Portugal. He came to Paris to study in 1527, some months
> before Ignatius. Juan de Polanco, who entered the Society in
> 1541 and became its longtime secretary in 1547, described
> Simão as "a man of desires" before he met Ignatius. The first
> draft of the *Formula of the Institute*, the Jesuit rule of life, contains
> the clause "Spiritu Sancto . . . impellente [with the Holy Spirit
> impelling them]," and refers to all of the companions. In the
> actual bull affirming the Society the words were changed to a

[11] The sequence in which the companions joined Ignatius is not altogether clear,
but what Rodrigues says of himself is believable. The *Memoriale, FN* 1:610, n. 138,
speaks of the companions' making the Exercises, but it is one thing to have made the
Exercises and then to have established a stable relationship with Ignatius, and another
thing to have become his companion before making the Exercises. *FN* 3:14[15].

passive form, "Spiritu Sancto . . . afflati [inspired by the Holy Spirit]." Here Simão expresses the general conviction of the companions that they were not driven by their own thoughts and desires but that the Holy Spirit was driving them along the path the Spirit had chosen for them.

[8] After these four the fifth in the course of the year was Father Diego Laínez, and a week after Laínez the sixth was Alfonso Salmerón, both of them Spaniards. Father Ignatius directed them very fruitfully along the path of God and they made so much progress with the divine help, that without knowing what the other was doing, each of them decided to renounce the seductions of the world, to sail to Jerusalem, and to choose the kind of life the others had already chosen. I mention the two of them together because they had both left Spain at the same time and came together to Paris to study, and both at almost the same time arrived at the same decision and embraced the same way of living.[12]

> *Commentary:* Laínez was born in 1512 at Almazán in Old Castile of a New Christian family, that is, of a Jewish family converted to Christianity. Salmerón was born in Toledo in 1515. They became friends in 1528 as students in Alcalá. Each was at the top of his class; Salmerón had a prodigious memory, Laínez great power in debate. Hearing much about Ignatius, in 1533 they decided to continue their studies in Paris and meet him there. Salmerón was only 18. When Paul III convened the Council of Trent in 1545, Faber, Laínez, and Salmerón were named papal theologians. Faber and Laínez had taught at the Sapienza in Rome, and all three had carried on theological disputations in the presence of the pope and various cardinals during dinner, so that they were familiar faces to Paul III. Faber, who was in Spain at the time, took sick on the return journey and died in Rome before reaching Trent.

[9] The seventh after the above two Fathers was Father Nicolás Bobadilla, a Spaniard. He also enjoyed a holy friendship with Ignatius and decided to embrace the same life as the others before he discovered what they were going to do. What happened to him happened to the other Fathers as well, for only after each one of them freely and of

---

[12] Laínez and Salmerón came to Paris in 1532 toward the end of the year, after the former had earned his Master of Arts in Alcalá. Each made the Exercises at the beginning of 1534. *GS* 205, *FN* 3:17[19].

his own accord had decided to dedicate himself wholly to the service of God and to the abovementioned way of life, then each one learned that the others had consecrated themselves to a similar way of living. When they learned this, words could not express how much joy, how much happiness, how much consolation and strength they experienced to persevere in their resolve.

> *Commentary:* Nicolás Alphonso was generally called Bobadilla after the village from which he came, Bobadilla del Camino, now known as Boadilla, near Palencia. He was born about 1509, studied rhetoric and logic in Valladolid, philosophy in Alcalá where he received his bachelor's degree in 1529, returned to Valladolid for theology, and in 1533 went to Paris to study languages. He was the last of the companions to die, at Loreto in 1590.

[10] Father Claude Jay, a Savoyard from the same town as Peter Faber or certainly from somewhere nearby, holds the eighth place among the others.[13] Adding him to the others happened this way. Faber returned home from Paris to take care of some business[14] and persuaded him to come to Paris to study more theology.[15] Claude was already a priest at that time and highly regarded by everyone and quietly living at home alone. I do not remember whether this Father had met Ignatius before the latter left Paris for Spain.[16] I do remember, however, that under Faber's direction he made much progress in the spiritual life so that not long after he came to the University of Paris, he became a companion to the first seven in what they proposed to do.[17]

> *Commentary:* Claude Jay was born about 1500. He was the first Jesuit to arrive at the Council of Trent, not as a papal theologian,

---

[13] Claude Jay was born in the valley of the Giffre river in Upper Savoy, in a place called Vulliets, now known as Vers les Jay, near to Mieussy, about 30 km. east of the city of Geneva, and the same distance north of Villaret, Faber's birthplace. *GS* 259, *FN* 3:18[22].

[14] Peter Faber returned to his country in 1533, saw Claude Jay and persuaded him to go to Paris to study. *FN* 3:18[23].

[15] Jay had studied, as had Faber a little later, in the town of LaRoche under a teacher named Velliard. On 28 March 1528 he was ordained a priest in Geneva. Later he ran a small college in the town of Faverges where Faber found him. *FN* 3:18[24].

[16] Jay went to Paris so as to enroll in the October 1534 courses. He had a room in the College of St. Barbara, where he undoubtedly knew Ignatius before the latter's departure for Spain in April 1535. *FN* 3:19[25].

[17] *FN* 1:183, 704. *FN* 3:19[26].

but as deputy for the Bishop of Augsburg, Otto Truchess von Waldburg.

[11] The ninth was Paschase Broët, a Frenchman and already a priest at that time, from the province commonly called Picardy. The tenth was Father John Codure from Provence. He was admitted into the number of the others a little before the Fathers left Paris and set out on their pilgrimage to Venice and Jerusalem. The Lord called these two to the Companionship of the above eight Fathers after Ignatius left Paris for Spain.[18] For this reason they had Father Faber as director for the Spiritual Exercises. This is the manner and the order that divine providence observed in gathering the first Fathers at the Society's beginning.

> *Commentary:* Broët was born in Bertrancourt, a town in northern France between Amiens and Arras. He would become the first Jesuit provincial of Italy and later the first provincial of France. Codure, on the other hand, was born in Seyne in southern France in 1508. He came to Paris about 1535. After the Society was approved in 1540, he was selected to help Ignatius in writing the *Constitutions*. The last to join the original group in Paris, he was the first to die, in 1541.

[18] Ignatius set out for Spain in April, 1535. *FN* 3:19[29].

CHAPTER TWO: Paris, 1534-36

The seven first Fathers persevered (for the others had not yet joined their company), and daily they became more and more inflamed with new desire and new zeal to carry out their resolve. And so they began to talk about the time when they would leave the confines of Paris and undertake some initiatives to carry out their hearts' desires. Since they had decided to give themselves completely to the salvation of their neighbor (after the Lord had brought them back from their pilgrimage to Jerusalem), it seemed good to study theology for three more years, and not to make a change in their exterior manner of living, but to persevere in the same manner as they had lived up to that time. It also seemed fitting that they should first commend to God for a time an undertaking that was both serious and arduous and involved great difficulties. They needed the breastplate of greater virtue before proceeding further in order to overcome obstacles and resist any other dangers likely to arise.

> *Commentary:* The vocabulary is that of knights preparing themselves to undertake great deeds in the service of their lord or their lady. To act otherwise would be to render them unworthy knights, as in the *Spiritual Exercises* 94. Cf. also *SpEx* 74.

[13] After long discussion, then, they decided that to give greater solidity to their determination, they would all bind themselves by a vow of poverty, of chastity, of sailing to Jerusalem, and on their return, with God's help, of working with all their might for the salvation of their neighbor, faithful and infidels alike, of preaching the divine word to everyone, and finally, of administering the holy sacraments of confession and Eucharist without any stipend.[1] The Fathers immediately made clear that they were not bound by the vow of poverty while they were studying in Paris, and that they could freely use whatever they needed [*viaticum*] for the Jerusalem pilgrimage.[2] They

---

[1] Cf. Mt. 10:8: "You received without payment; give without payment."

[2] *Viaticum* means traveling money, provisions for a journey, money made by a soldier in war, savings, prize money, money to pay the expenses for one studying abroad (*Harper's Latin Dictionary*, p. 1984c). The Church applied the word to a final Eucharist for one dying.

vowed besides that they would never accept anything for celebrating Mass, at the same time openly admitting that accepting a stipend for Masses or other liturgical ceremonies was quite legitimate. For themselves, however, in order to embrace poverty and evangelical perfection more closely, they wanted to rid themselves voluntarily even of legitimate things, so that they might avoid as far as possible the malicious lies of heretics, despoiling them of the opportunity of claiming that they were acting under the pretense of piety in order to make greater profit and become wealthier and more affluent.

> *Commentary:* The attitude of the companions in the above two paragraphs is similar to that of worthy knights in the Middle Ages; their activity is similar to that of the early Christians in Acts:
>> "They devoted themselves to the apostles' teaching and fellowship, to the breaking of bread and the prayers. . . . All who believed were together and had all things in common; they would sell their possessions and goods and distribute the proceeds to all, as any had need. . . . Now the whole group of those who believed were of one heart and soul" (Acts 2:42, 44, 4:32).

[14] Because some of them ardently desired to bring the light of evangelical truth to unbelievers, they began to talk about that. Because all of them were determined in an extraordinary manner to pour out their lives in constancy, if need be, for any reason at all relating to the greater worship and reverence of God, they all came to the same conclusion, some more ardently and some less enflamed according to the measure of Christ's gift [Eph. 4:7]. These vows, moreover, of propagating the faith of Christ, by unanimous agreement were tempered in such a way that all would sail for Jerusalem and there they would commend the matter once more to God. If at that time, they said, this decision is confirmed by a majority, we shall seize the opportunity divinely offered to us. For what better or more proper thing can be offered? But if the majority reject the decision, then all of us will return without breaking up the group.[3] It was also decided that if within

---

[3] They were not agreed on their way of living after the pilgrimage. Some, apparently Ignatius, Laínez, and Xavier, were inclined toward staying in the Holy Land; others, like Faber and Rodrigues, it seems, preferred to return to Europe and place them-

the course of a year after their arrival in Venice they could not sail to Jerusalem after making every effort to do so, they would be released from that vow and would make their way to Rome (which is what they would have done if they came back from Jerusalem), throw themselves at the feet of the Supreme Pontiff, share with him their thoughts and declare that their lives were consecrated to the salvation of the human race, and finally suppliantly implore him what advice he would give in this matter as Pontiff. And if under divine inspiration he approved what they wanted to do, then in order to carry out their plan better they would request unrestricted faculties to preach, hear confessions, and celebrate the Eucharist anywhere in the world. Moreover they would make every effort to make the Supreme Pontiff understand that they were ready at his command to proclaim the Good News of Christ without any hesitation throughout the whole world, even in lands subject to the Turks or other tyrants who abhorred the Christian religion. These, Very Reverend Father, were the first lineaments of our Society. This vow was first made, if I recall correctly, in 1534 on August 15, the feast of the Blessed Virgin Mary's Assumption, for in this matter all the Fathers took the Virgin as our helper and protector and special intercessor before her Son Jesus Christ our Lord, taking as an intercessor also the blessed martyr Denis at whose holy shrine these vows were first taken.

> *Commentary:* Once more the companions are like knights setting out on a Crusade or in search of the Holy Grail. Jesus is their Lord and Mary is their Lady. They have pledged themselves at the shrine of St. Denis and have chosen him as their intercessor. But they are also like the apostles. Just before Jesus's ascension, he said to the apostles, "But you will receive power when the Holy Spirit will come upon you; and you will be my witnesses in Jerusalem, and in all Judea and Samaria, and to the ends of the earth" (Acts 1:8).

---

selves under obedience to the Roman Pontiff. Finally, the ultimate judgment on this matter was delayed until their arrival in Jerusalem, and was to be decided by a plurality of votes. *FN* 3:22⁶. Polanco agrees with this in three different writings, but in a fourth remarks, "Their intent was that after visiting the holy places they would go amongst the infidels and spend their lives on their behalf, if God would be served, or meet death for the divine glory; since it had not turned out that way the first time, Father Ignatius was going to try it a second time." *FN* 2:310.

[15] They decided that the place to take these vows should be the chapel of St. Denis, which is situated halfway up the Mount of Martyrs [Montmartre] about a kilometer[4] from the city, solitary, removed from all disturbance, and far from crowds of people. To offer their holocaust to God more fervently,[5] they prepared themselves by fasting, meditating on divine things, expiating their sins, and other means of mortification. When they confirmed this vow on the same day and in the same place and with the same ceremony the two following years, Father Ignatius was not present[6] for certain reasons, but they did everything following his counsel and judgment. I doubt also whether in the second year Father Claude Jay was present to confirm the vow, but he was present the third and final time along with the other two Fathers who joined the rest later.[7]

> *Commentary:* Although the chapel was that of St. Denis, the church housing the chapel was called St. Mary, and the day was the Feast of the Assumption. The fasting and praying and expiating sins is not unlike the program Ignatius followed at Montserrat: fasting for three days before confessing his sins, spending the night before Mary's feast of the Annunciation in vigil before the statue of Our Lady, hanging up his sword at her shrine and clothing himself in pilgrim garb. Amadis of Gaul had also spent the night in vigil before a statue of Mary. The companions were preparing to carry out their "propositum" or firm determination to pilgrimage to Jerusalem and work for the salvation of the whole world.

[16] No outsider was present, just the Fathers. Father Faber celebrated Mass, and before he gave Communion to his companions, he turned to them and held the sacred host in his hands. They were kneeling on the floor with their minds fixed on God, and each in his own turn pronounced the vows in a clear voice that was audible to all.

---

[4] Rodrigues uses Roman miles in the Latin text and Portuguese leagues in the Portuguese version. The translation attempts to approximate these in kilometers or miles without pretending to be exact.

[5] Portuguese: "So that they could more fervently make this sacrifice which they wanted to offer of their persons to God."

[6] Understand this of the renovation of vows in 1535 and 1536. Ignatius left for Spain in April 1535 and then went to Italy to wait for the companions. *FN* 3:25[11].

[7] It seems that Jay was there both years. He came in 1534 and shortly after made the Exercises under Faber (see [10] above). *FN* 3:25[12].

Then they all received holy communion together. Turning to the altar, Father, in the same way, before consuming the life-giving bread, pronounced his vows so distinctly and clearly that he was heard by everyone.[8]

> *Commentary:* This ceremony, placed immediately preceding communion rather than immediately after the reading of the Gospel, reflects the companions' emphasis on the Eucharist even though their commitment after pilgrimaging to Jerusalem is to preach the Gospel. The vows are addressed to Jesus in a profoundly ecclesial context: the Eucharist held in the hand of a priest who represents Jesus, for they could not in any way separate Jesus from the Church. They swear their commitment to their liege Lord as though placing their hands in his after the manner of medieval vassals.

[17] Here I would dare to say this to Your Reverend Paternity: those first Fathers of the Society, who at that moment truly committed themselves to God with their whole heart, offered that holocaust with such eagerness, with such abnegation of will, with such hope in the divine mercy, that often, when I think about it afterwards, a passionate burning fills my heart, a new flood of devotion swells up, and I experience incredible awe. Unending thanks and eternal praise to God for his wonderful gifts to us, because he was mindful of us and showed us his mercy [Tobit 8:18].

> *Commentary:* Rodrigues presents Montmartre as a kind of new Pentecost, a human transformation, a manifestation of the wonderful works of God [*magnalia Dei*], "God's deeds of power" (Acts 2:11). The reference to Tobit is startling, strong evidence that Montmartre was a major event in each of their lives and in their existence as a group. The final words are from the prayer of Tobias after the extraordinary experience of successfully spending his wedding night with Sara who had already lost six bridegrooms in a row to death on her wedding nights, "It has

[8] The Latin reads: "tunc sacram *simul* receperunt synaxim" (italics added). The sequence of actions seems to be (1) each one pronounced his vows; (2) Faber gave each one communion under the form of bread; (3) Faber turned around and faced the altar, pronounced his vows, and received communion under both species. It is unlikely that he gave communion to each man immediately after the man vowed, for the ritual expressed both their individual commitment and their commitment as a group.

not turned out as I expected, but you have dealt with us according to your great mercy." Montmartre was a risky venture, as was Pentecost.

[18] When the ceremony was over, the Fathers spent the rest of the day near the spring (where St. Denis is said to have carried his head after it had been cut off, and washed off the blood that was gushing forth). It is situated at the foot of the mountain[9] across from that little chapel where they had taken their vows. With great joy and happiness they talked together about that zeal for the divine service with which they were on fire. At last, when the sun was already setting, they made their way home praising and glorifying God.

> *Commentary:* The memories stirring in Rodrigues in 1577 are not the result of mere nostalgia; a chord deep in his heart has been struck, as it had been struck before. On 20 August 1566, 32 years after their vows at Montmartre, words come tumbling in a rush from his pen as he writes to Nicolás Bobadilla:
>
>> Very Reverend Father in Christ, the peace of Christ. On the eve of our Lady in August of 1566, on coming from saying Mass and from commending Your Reverence to God, and having passed that whole morning in recalling what we had done that day at Montmartre and in his vineyards, and coming, as I say, from Mass to my room, there on my desk was a letter from Your Reverence of 18 June of this same year, written at Our Lady of Loreto, which brought me so much consolation that I took it as almost a miracle to receive a letter from Your Reverence on that day in the midst of the preceding thoughts. And may our Lord be pleased that you remembered me, for certainly, although sometimes I am not present to what I ought to be, nevertheless, whether present or absent I hold Your Reverence in my heart, and I love you most dearly, and I wish to demonstrate this desire more by deeds than I have done up to now; and if I am unable to do more, let the desire stand for the fact. It would

---

[9] This spring was situated where a dead-end street is now found, the Impasse Girardon (Rue Girardon, 5), not to be confused with a nearby spring, Fontaine du Buc, which is no longer in existence. *GS* 215[180]. See *FN* 3:27[16].

give me boundless consolation if Your Reverence would write to me even now and then.

And now, for sure, we are so few in numbers [Salmerón was the only other companion still living] that our love grows much more, and may Your Reverence inform me in detail what you are doing and how you are. I have also received much consolation from the great progress of the Society in those parts, and it cannot cease to be like that in view of the gentle way of proceeding of blessed Father Francis [Borgia]. May God grant him much life and health.

Things around here are going well: I am the only one who profits little from the good opportunities that God has given me; nevertheless, I hope in Our Lord that since he has begun to show me his favor, he may bring it to perfection: he will bring it about in eternity. My bodily health is better; but in the end, I am on my way to the border crossing.

May Your Reverence let me know about Father Salmerón, for I also have a great desire to know about his health. I console myself much in thinking that all of us have to go (and can't delay for long) before the one who called us to go to Montmartre. I do not know whether we shall see each other again in this life, but, as Your Reverence says, let us see each other by letters, and may God Our Lord do with us what is most for his service.

From Toledo, 20 August 1566. Your Reverence's servant in Christ, Simão. (*EB* 734-35).

Bobadilla, too, was deeply affected by Montmartre. Addressing Fr. General Francis Borgia on 31 August 1569, 35 years after Montmartre, he writes exuberantly:

Very Reverend Father in Christ. The grace and peace of Christ the Lord be always with us. Amen. It was not without deep significance that Your Reverend Paternity wrote the long letter you sent me from Frascati, written on the feast of the Assumption of Our Lady the Virgin Mary to whom I am dearly devoted, for on that day our Company had its beginnings at Montmartre near Paris, where ten of us made the first vows to go to Jerusalem. This holy feast is the root and origin of the Company: "Look to Abraham your father and to Sara who bore you," said God through the prophet [Is. 51:2] recalling the father and mother from whom they descended. We of the Company ought to do the same, especially those of us who were there [and] whom Christ and his holy Mother took as their sons and as fathers of this great Company. Blessed be God and his holy Mother forever and ever. Amen. . . Christ, in the Gospel of the Assumption of his holy Mother, says that Mary has chosen the best part [Lk. 10:42] and that Martha was solicitous about many things [Lk 10:41]. Then who would refuse the best, that Your Reverend Paternity offers and gives me, which is a paradise in this life and the beginning of the paradise of perpetual glory? May Christ, the Son of Mary, lead us to this glory where they reign body and soul in eternal repose, towards which all of us are walking, sighing until we get there. Amen. So be it. So be it. . . . I remain asking Christ and Holy Mary, his Mother, for Your Reverend Paternity's happiness, with all the saints, that you direct all things to the glory of Christ and the good of the whole Company. Amen. May all go very well. From Nola, the end of August 1569. Your Very Reverend Paternity's son in Christ, Bobadilla. (*MB* 498.)

What a momentous occasion Montmartre was for the first companions is further manifest in the letter of Bobadilla to Father General Claude Aquaviva on 11 August 1589 as sole survivor of the original group 54 years after the event:

Very Reverend Father in Christ, the peace of Christ. Recalling (as I often do) this holy feast of the Assumption of the glorious Madonna, especially in my old age [he was born about 1509], I cannot fail to write to Your Very Reverend Paternity, in view of the fact that on this day at Montmartre near Paris the first Fathers of our Company made a vow to go to Jerusalem. The "great deep" [Ps. 36:6] of Divine providence commuted that vow to another better and more fruitful vow of pilgrimaging in religion and has scattered the Society all over the world. Blessed be Jesus Christ. Amen.

As for my life, it is more death than life: I do not
sleep well; I can't eat since I have no teeth; catarrh and
pains are not lacking throughout my body, and after
eighty there is more "toil and trouble" [Ps. 90:10]; the
remedy is patience. Recommending myself to God
and his angels and blessed saints in heaven, and begging the Company and others to pray for me, and that
all who know and see me may have compassion on
me and be kind to me and help me both spiritually
and corporally so that what little remains of my pilgrimage may come to an end to the glory of Christ
Our Lord so that I can say with the glorious Madonna,
"in all these I sought rest, and I shall abide in the
inheritance of the Lord"[Ecclesiasticus 24:11 (Douay)],
with Christ the Lord at my side who with God the
Father and the Holy Spirit lives and reigns world
without end. Amen. And may you be well with the
Father Assistants, the house and college. Amen. From
Cacciabella, 11 August 1589. Father Horatio and
Dionysius send greetings to Your Very Reverend
Paternity. Bobadilla. (*FN* 3:320--21.)

[19] After the Fathers began to talk among themselves about entering
upon this way of life they judged that the frequentation of the sacraments should always be linked with their scholarly studies. And so,
on every Sunday and on the major feasts of the year they would
cleanse their consciences and receive the Body of Christ. By their comments and by their example many students and many of the people of
Paris were led to frequent the same sacraments. When the savage
enemy of the human race[10] saw what they had done, he was enflamed
by the revolutionary nature of this approach, and perhaps conjectur-
ing that he was going to lose no small amount because of it, he persuaded some of the Spanish students to report the name of Ignatius to
the Inquisitor of the city. Deceived by some false arguments and
deluded by excessive zeal, they go to the judge and say that they think
that the poison of contagious false doctrine is being spread secretly by
Ignatius, but they do not assert anything as certain. The Inquisitor

---

[10] In the Spiritual Exercises, "enemy of the human race" is the name Ignatius gives
the evil spirit who often tries to insert confusion where good has been accomplished,
sowing weeds among the wheat.

diligently investigates the matter. He finds that they are totally in error and that good and holy meditations on divine things are being taught by Ignatius. From that event he takes the opportunity of striking up a friendship with Ignatius and the other companions, and after that he always loved them.[11]

> *Commentary:* So also in Acts "the priests, the captain of the temple, and the Sadducees . . . were annoyed . . . so they arrested them," and brought them before the "rulers, elders, and scribes" who questioned them, and they responded in such a manner that "they were amazed" (Acts 4:1-13).

[20] This suffering later produces a great reward. For some years later, when a great storm of false accusations arose in Rome, one charge that was made against the Fathers (which I shall deal with later in more detail at the proper time)[12] was this one, that our men were fugitives and had left Paris because of the crime of heresy. But by the immense mercy of God who is wont to provide wisely in all matters, it happened that the Inquisitor from Paris was in Rome at the time. When he was asked to testify accurately on the matter, he said many things in favor of the Fathers. He told how he had used great diligence to investigate their life and character,[13] and finally he testified in detail about their innocence, about their integrity of life and their commitment to the true religion, and he affirmed that they were so far from the suspicion of heresy that even when they departed they all left in Paris a great longing after them.

> *Commentary:* The providence of God is a theme that runs all through Simão's narrative. The experience of the companions is reflected in the opening clause of the Preamble to the *Constitutions:* "[134] Although God our Creator and Lord is the one who in his Supreme Wisdom and Goodness must preserve, direct, and carry forward in his divine service this least Society

---

[11] The accusation against Ignatius was made to the inquisitor, Fr. Valentine Liévin, shortly before Ignatius set out for Spain; for this reason Ignatius wanted a verdict as soon as possible. When the inquisitor agreed, Ignatius brought a scribe and witnesses to him. In their presence the inquisitor praised Ignatius and asked for a copy of the Exercises. *GS* 244. See [85] below. *FN* 3:28[20].

[12] See below [87]. *FN* 3:29[21].

[13] It was not Valentine Liévin who came to Rome in 1538 but Matthew Ory, who had passed judgment concerning Ignatius in Paris in 1529. *FN* 3:29[22].

of Jesus, just as he deigned to begin it; . . ." and again in the opening sentence of Part X of the *Constitutions*: "[812] The Society was not instituted by human means; and it is not through them that it can be preserved and increased, but through the grace of the omnipotent hand of Christ our God and Lord."

[21] Meanwhile Ignatius suffered from poor health, and was especially troubled by stomach pains. Therefore, following the advice of doctors and the encouragement of his companions, he was constrained to return to Spain to see if a change of place and the air of his native land would restore his health, for if he stayed as he was he would be incapable of anything in the future. The companions mourned the fact that their Father was gone, as was right, but because of his absence their burning desire to persevere in their vows did not grow cold. For their hope and strength was placed in God. For just as each one by himself, freely, before he had heard of the vocation or determination of any other, began to aspire to this one pattern of living, so each one firmly decided within himself that, even if the others defected, he would put his hand to the plow and not look back (Lk. 9:62). And so Father Ignatius returned to Spain more than a year before the Fathers left Paris, and after recovering his health somewhat, he left Spain and came to Venice to await the Fathers there as they had decided.[14]

[22] The scheduled day was now approaching for putting an end to their theological studies and leaving the city, when the companions learned from a letter of Ignatius that he had already arrived in Venice. They decided that the date set for their departure from Paris, January 25, 1537, the feast of St. Paul's conversion, should be canceled and advanced to November 15, 1536. They thought the time should be advanced in this way because they believed there would be necessary delays because of the difficulties and dangers inherent in the journey. Passes from France into Italy and other places were closed because of a terrible war between the kings of France and Spain brought on by our sins.[15]

[14] Ignatius left for Spain in April 1535; the companions left Paris on 15 November 1536. Ignatius left Spain for Italy toward the end of 1535 to wait for them there. *FN* 3:30[25].

[15] In 1536, after King Francis I of France had occupied Savoy and Turin, war broke out between him and Emperor Charles V, who invaded Provence. See *GS* 264-69 for more details. Since these territories were astir with war, the companions were forced to take a more difficult route through Lorraine, Germany, and Switzerland. See below [25]. *FN* 3:31[27].

[23] Before setting out the Fathers approach two outstanding scholars, each a professor with a doctorate, in order to outline the nature of the way of life they had determined upon; they praise it, approve it, extol it; they also point out that it is fraught with difficulties and dangers. Another professor with a doctorate, to be commended for his holiness and learning, who heard that Father Faber's departure from Paris was imminent, knowing nothing of the other companions, said to him, "Is this true what I hear of you, Faber? Are you quitting Paris? Will you leave Paris bereft of your great talent? I for one am convinced that you cannot leave here without grave sin, since you are depriving many people of a sure cure and are putting your energy into the uncertain salvation of other people. Don't think I say this lightly, for if you wish, I shall gather together all the arguments." But divine providence had decreed something far different.

> *Commentary:* Another attraction capable of distracting a person from a call that comes from God is that of other vocations, other ways of living in which one can serve God. In Acts 5:34-39 Gamaliel stresses the conflict that can exist between the human way of viewing things and God's way of viewing them. The companions wisely seek confirmation of their decision by consulting competent persons capable of grasping both the advantages and disadvantages in the course they are taking. Even the thoughtful objections of another learned and holy man, expressed in the strongest terms possible, contribute to confirming the decision, for those objections had to be taken very seriously and weighed very carefully. The companions were viewing matters from God's perspective, not walking blindly into a trap.

[24] It also happened at the same time while the Fathers were preparing to depart that an unexpected messenger arrived from Pamplona for Xavier who announced that he had been elected a canon of the Church of Pamplona. Now this might have upset an unstable and inconstant person, but he already considered this and greater honors to be worthless.[16] This is what I can say briefly about the beginnings of the Society in Paris, entrusting all of it to the judgment of those who remember the events better.

---

[16] See *GS* 270-72. Xavier wrote a letter to the cathedral chapter of Pamplona declining the honor. *EX* 1:13-14.

Commentary: Francis Xavier had, indeed, envisioned the life of a canon as a possibility for him and had applied for the position. It was a position suitable for a nobleman, attractive for the dignity and remuneration attached to the office. Francis's priorities had changed, as had those of all of the companions, and he experienced no difficulty in giving up a once-coveted position.

CHAPTER THREE: Paris to Venice, 1536-37

[25] It seemed extremely difficult for Spaniards to cross through France when two very powerful monarchs were waging a fierce war against each other. Nevertheless, after some consideration it seemed safer to leave France for the Duchy of Lorraine, which was not at odds with either France or Spain but joined to each by a treaty of friendship. This area bordered France on one side, Belgium on another, and Switzerland on a third. The Fathers decided to enter Germany by taking this route along which both Spaniards and Frenchmen could travel. It was long, but a little safer. The space to cover between Paris and Italy was shaped like a half-moon or two sides of a triangle: after traveling one leg, another leg still remained to be covered. Forced by necessity, they set out on that long but somewhat safer journey.[1]

[26] This is how the Fathers set out from Paris, dressed in the long, well-worn clothing of students from the University of Paris. They held staffs in their hands and wore broad-brimmed hats on their heads. Hanging from their shoulders was a leather knapsack in which they kept a Bible, a breviary, and assorted writing materials. Around their necks hung rosaries for all eyes to see, and the skirts of their ample garments were tucked into their cinctures lest they get tangled in their feet. On the day they set out after entrusting themselves completely to

[1] They left Paris on 15 November 1536 and arrived in Venice on 8 January 1537. They traveled about 50 km. per day. The reconstructed route, partially certain and partially probable: 15 Nov. departure from Paris; 16 Nov. Meaux, 45 km.; 17 Nov. Château Thierry; 18 Epernay, 142 km.; 20 Sainte-Menehoulde, 200 km.; 22 Verdun, 245 km.; 23-25 Metz, 300 km. (stayed 3 days); 25 Pont-à-Mousson, 330 km.; 26 Nancy, 358 km.; Saint-Nicolas-du-Port, 371 km.; Luneville; 27 Blamont, 420 km.; Saarburg; 28 Zabern, 470 km.; 29 Strasbourg, 520 km.; 3 Dec. Basel, 130 km. from Strasbourg (3 days of rest); Rheinfelden; Frick, 35 km.; Brugg, 50 km.; Baden, 60 km.; Kaiserstuhl [?], 75 km.; Winterthur, 110 km.; Frauenfeld, 130 km.; Pfyn, 140 km.; Weinfelden, 155 km.; Constance, 175 km. After Constance the only name in the documents is Trent. The road along the upper side of Lake Constance goes through Meersburg, 10 km.; about 9 Dec. Lindau, 50 km., the last Protestant city on the companions' pilgrimage; Bregenz; Feldkirch, probably Reschen-Scheideck; Merano; Bolzano; Trent, then apparently through Valsugana, Bassano or less probably Feltre, then to Castelfranco, Mestre, Venice, 170 km. from Trent. *FN* 3:32[2], drawn from data in *GS* 277-96.

[2] *GS* 277-96 takes the companions from Paris to Venice. He does not translate the text of Rodrígues but follows it closely, generally omitting Simon's tales about himself.

faith in God and surrendering to the grace of God, they began their journey rejoicing as though celebrating a feast, so filled with joy that their feet hardly seemed to touch the ground.[3]

[27] About five or six days earlier some of the companions had left in order to wait at Meldis (commonly called Meaux, if I am not mistaken) for the rest who had stayed in Paris to give what remained of their belongings to the poor. This city is, I think, twenty-nine miles from Paris.[4] While staying there on the first night of the journey one of the Fathers found a large, bloody blister on his shoulder, so that the very sight of it caused fearful horror. That whole night he moaned and groaned, twisting and turning on the ground where he lay, deeply saddened, fearing that this blister would keep him from making the journey. But when the sun rose and it was time to leave the Father checked and not only found no blister but not even a trace of it.[5]

> *Commentary:* From the consolation of [26] Rodrigues is plunged
> into the temptation of desolation in [27]. Can he make the jour-
> ney? The question is similar to the one that troubled Ignatius at
> Manresa after determining on a life of asceticism, "How will
> you be able to endure this life for the seventy years you have to
> live?" (*Autobiography*, 20). To place this experience at the start of
> the journey suggests that Rodrigues is giving it as an example
> of the sorts of questions that must have arisen in each of their
> hearts many times on the journey. "It is characteristic of God
> and his angels . . . to give genuine happiness and spiritual joy

[3] Juan Polanco, who entered the Society in 1541, became its Secretary in 1547. Wanting to know more about its origins, he asked Diego Laínez to write him a letter bringing him up to date. The latter replied from Bologna on June 16, 1547. The original is in Spanish; an early Latin translation accompanies the text in the *Monumenta, FN* 1:70-145 [1-62]. For simplicity's sake references to this text will be in brackets with L and the paragraph number, here [L33]. From that letter we glean a few more stories about the period covered by Rodrigues. Laínez indicates that on this journey the three priests said Mass every day, and the others confessed and received communion, also that it rained almost every day in France, and in Germany they struggled through snow.

[4] A distance of 45km. *GS* 277[1,17] refers to Charles Estienne's *Guide des Chemins de France de 1553* (Routes 60, 69, 74, 88): from Paris through Pantin, Bondy, Villeparisis, through the woods of Parisis, Claye-Souilly, then across the Bevronne and along the Marne to Meaux (Route 60).

[5] Rodrigues tells this story about himself. *FN* 3:35[5]..

. . . It is characteristic of the enemy to fight against this happiness and spiritual consolation, by using specious reasonings, subtleties, and persistent deceits" (*SpEx* 329). The conflict between the companions and the evil spirit has begun.

[28] At this point, most Reverend Father, you will grant me permission to depart a bit from my purpose and make a little speech about an event that was a source of grace and of wonderment. In the city of Meaux the Fathers were waiting for their companions. Meanwhile out of devotion they usually went almost every day to the cell of St. Fiacre, about a mile and three quarters outside the city. St. Fiacre, so they say, was the son and heir of some English king, but on fire with love for the eternal king he left the land for faraway places (so that when friends looked for him he could not be found). There, all alone and unknown to anyone, he lived a life of great poverty. He finally came to this place where, begging from door to door, he gradually withdrew into a woods dense then with trees, and now made noble by the cell he created there. There while preparing to make a little cell for himself sometime out of logs, he traces out the spot with the staff he used to lean on. The thick trees, torn up by the roots, easily fall into place after the one tracing the lines. A little old lady, seeing this marvel by chance, screams and yells and calls the man a great wonder-worker. Fiacre, sorry that he had been seen, sits down on a very hard rock which provided a comfortable seat for him just as though it were soft and sandy. (I saw the rock, and a trace of the seat still remains.) Sitting there he asks the Lord that since it was not permissible during his life, no woman would have access to the place where he would be buried. And so today, in the very place he had once chosen as a home for himself, he lies in a chapel enclosed by an iron grill, lest ordinary women would inadvertently step in, a step they could not take back, for it is well known that this happens frequently to many who enter a place without regard to prohibitions.[6]

---

[6] St. Fiacre is claimed by both the Scots and the Irish as their countryman. He crossed into Gaul in the sixth century, was welcomed by Bishop Faro of Meaux, and lived as a hermit in a forest nearby. Women were strictly forbidden to approach his cell, which became a place of pilgrimage. He worked many miracles both in life and after death, and was especially solicitous for the poor. He died about 670. As patron of gardeners, he is often pictured with a shovel. Horse-drawn cabs in Paris took the name of "fiacres" from being started from a hotel with a statue of St. Fiacre above the door. See *The Book of Saints*, compiled by the Benedictine Monks of St. Augustine's Abbey, Ramsgate (New York: Macmillan, 1938), 111. According to another account, the legend was that Bishop Faro had promised him the area he could dig a ditch around in a day. Fiacre simply drew a line in the dirt with his staff and the ditch obligingly dug itself!

Commentary: The companions were more inclined to find the miraculous around every corner than many in the post-modern era. What is more important, they were skilled at finding God in all things and events. They also more easily tolerated manifestations of misogyny as an integral part of their culture. Misogyny was as destructive then as it is now, but men and women today are more likely to be aware that it is an ugly blot on contemporary culture. Father General Peter-Hans Kolvenbach's call for creative fidelity to the Society of Jesus's way of living is a call to Jesuits to be faithful in a creative manner to the Society's virtues in the past, not its defects.

[29] But let us get back to the matter at hand. The remaining companions leave Paris after distributing their surplus to the poor. After about a day's journey, near an inn a bit set off from the road, some farmers and French soldiers are watching the approaching travelers, and noticing the way they are dressed, say to them, "Who are you? Where are you from? Where are you going?" The Spaniards remain silent, and the French companions respond, "We are students from Paris." Still one of the soldiers insists, "What country do you come from? Are you Carmelites, monks, surely clergy? Look, come over here, for we have to know who you are." But an old woman who was there addresses the soldiers, "Let them go," she says, "let the men go, for they are going off to convert some province." They laugh, and the Fathers continue the journey they had begun. In crossing France, the French Fathers always respond to questioners, mainly in a few words in their own dialect, answering for the Spaniards (except for two Spaniards who spoke French fluently).[7] Whenever the question of birthplace came up, the French immediately respond with their own birthplace. Interrogated individually, the Spaniards say that they are students from Paris. With these answers everything was so covered that it does not come to light that Spaniards are in the group. Once when one of the Spaniards who spoke French fluently was walking with a French soldier and the soldier asked him privately where he came from, "I am a student," he replies. The soldier insists, "The question is about your homeland. Where are you from?" The Father repeats the same answer. Fed up, the soldier says, "Bah! Stupid ox! I know that." And leaving him immediately, he stomped off.

[7] One of the two Spaniards was certainly Xavier, the other perhaps Laínez. *FN* 3:38[10].

[30] After they all gathered joyfully at Meaux, they began to discuss a few matters. First of all, whether indications favored pilgrimaging in poverty after leaving Meaux, begging alms from door to door. Or would it be better to keep enough money to get to Venice (for they found that they still had a little). Then, should they all travel together, or go in two groups, or two by two? So they commended the questions to God, and after confessing their sins and receiving communion, they decided that they would go by foot as previously determined, that in place of alms they should take as much money as they thought necessary for the trip to Venice, and that they would not divide into groups. They had to journey through heretical territory; it was wintertime and all the roads were clogged with snow; it could happen that they would be delayed on their journey or delayed in reaching their goal because of the cold weather or sickness or danger. After making these decisions, they left Meaux, grateful to God. On the journey they spend all or a good part of the time in prayer, with sighs and cries to God, and in other prayerful meditations. To those asking where they are going, they reply: to the shrine of St. Nicholas in Lorraine, a place famous for attracting large crowds for religious reasons, and to which they themselves had to go.[8]

[31] They had gone hardly two or three days from Meaux flushed with joy and showing their happiness at getting started on their journey, when two young men, spurring their horses, finally catch up with them.[9] As soon as these two had heard that the companions had departed, they left Paris. One of the young men was blood brother of one of the companions.[10] The other was not only from the same country and people but was closely bound to the same companion by their

---

[8] Saint-Nicholas-du-Port, on the bank of the Meurthe River. It was begun in 1495 and finished in 1553. *FN* 3:40[11]. It underwent a complete renovation at the end of the twentieth century, and now contains a chapel celebrating the visit of the companions.

[9] See *GS* 281[21-22] for Estienne's route from Meaux. The first day would have taken them along the Marne valley to Trilport, across the Marne, through a forest to Saint-Jean-les-deux-Jumeaux, across the Marne again at Fay to La Ferté-sous-Juarre, across again at Luzancy to Méry-sur-Marne, along the right bank to Crouttes and Charly, through the forest of la Harguc to Mont-de Bonneil, then past the Augustinian abbey of Essommes to Château-Thierry (Route 69). The second day would take them to Paroy, Sauvigny, across the Marne to Dormans, Port-à-Binson, La Cave, Boursault, Mardeuil, Épernay (Route 74), about 31 miles.

[10] Sebastião Rodrigues, Simão's brother. The meeting could have taken place between Dormans and Épernay. *GS, ibid.*

long-standing friendship. So they approached the companion and interrogate him: where is he going? What is on his mind? What is he trying to do? They bring up the dangers in these turbulent times. They try every argument they can to change his mind. The brother tries to frighten his brother off from the course he has undertaken. The friend tries to convert his friend. Each warns him in the same way: he should look at what he is doing, should reflect carefully, should avoid anything rash; they insist vigorously that he should not disrupt the course of his life, should not waste prodigally the future in store for him, should not throw himself on the incontrovertible spears of indigence, infamy, and ignominy, or expose himself to the stress of so many hardships and perils. Why so much? Finally they bring out every trick to wear him down that a beloved brother and a dear friend can muster. On the other hand, the companion tries to convert both of them to share his way of life, but just as he was not able to be called back from what he had determined to do, so also they could not be torn away from their way of life. Finally the two young men give up on the companion and in deep distress return to Paris. The companions, their enthusiasm unabated, continue on their way.[11]

> *Commentary:* Even fundamental blessings of life, the bonds of family and the bonds of friendship, can also become inordinate attachments if not kept in proper perspective. The story illustrates that each of the companions had to deal with family ties and friendships, and each did it in response to the grace given to each.

[32] On this journey they picked up the habit of going down on their knees in sight of everyone when they entered an inn, giving thanks to God for the gifts they had received, and especially that they had arrived safe and sound. Likewise, when they left they went on their knees to beg God for a favorable journey and for God's help and favor in everything, and then they would set out. Their action stirred those in the inn to great admiration, especially the heretics in Germany. The latter, astonished at seeing these foreigners who were speaking a different language and were dressed differently, were quick to call in

---

[11] *GS*281[24] (following Estienne): after reaching Épernay the companions would cross the Marne to Ay (probably not detouring past Châlons-sur-Marne), Les Grandes Loges, across the Nesle River and the Rheims-Chalons road to Saint-Remy-sur-Bussy, Sainte-Menehould, across the Aisne to Verrières, through the Argonne forest to Clermont-en-Argonne, across the Aisne again to Verdun (Route 88), about 62 miles.

people fluent in Latin. And if these were more hard hearted, stiff-necked, and more obstinate, they would immediately provoke our men to a disputation on matters of faith. They not only did not refuse, but even under the threat of serious danger they consistently showed that their sect was false, vain, and good for nothing. They had decided to do this even if they were charged with a capital crime. This happened over and over again and therefore it would take a long time to tell the tale, but since I am determined to be brief, to make a long story short, I shall omit it.

> *Commentary:* The *Formula of the Institute*, written by the companions in 1539, speaks of "the propagation of the faith," which they certainly had as their goal in going to Jerusalem to live among the Jews and Muslims, both of which they called "infidels." The Formula had in mind as well the conversion of "heretics." The companions clearly do not anticipate by centuries the more irenic ecumenical decrees of Vatican II. At that time neither side showed openness to the other, a willingness to listen and to understand what the other side was saying or trying to say. The companions had a difficult time practicing the admonition at the beginning of the *Spiritual Exercises* to give another's words the best interpretation possible (*SpEx* 22). Nonetheless they learned from their experiences along the way.

[33] Since they were passing beyond the French border,[12] as though saying a last farewell to France, they cleansed their consciences and received the most holy Body of Christ. Then after dinner a French nobleman came to them with a large body of armed men; after they responded well to his bitter attack on the Roman Catholic faith, he departed.

[34] When they reached the border of Lorraine, the companions faced their greatest danger. They were very much afraid that the Spaniards would be recognized, indeed robbed and taken prisoner. At this time that region was swarming with French troops who had broken into a Belgian province through this section of Lorraine. After making many raids, they furiously attack at random, now here, now there, so that with all the chaos even natives of Lorraine did not dare to go anywhere. Everyone was amazed that the Fathers were able to evade the

---

[12] *GS* 281[25]: Sainte-Menehould, about 36 miles from Épernay.

military who, with loose reins and no religious fear, were pillaging wherever greed and sheer nerve invited them to satisfy their lusts. Once they came upon troops of an entire army at Metz (as my memory serves me).[13] The gates were barred and all the entrances well fortified, closed to the licentiousness of the military. They were finally admitted with great difficulty as students from Paris who were making their way directly to the shrine of St. Nicholas[14] for religious reasons, along with some farmers who were leaving their fields and farms and fleeing from the wanton boldness of soldiers on the rampage. They were in this town for three days until the soldiers were sent elsewhere. From there they set out to visit the sacred religious shrine of St. Nicholas.[15] This shrine is almost at the far end of Lorraine bordering on Germany. But the people of this city said that the Fathers had not come by land but had clearly flown down from heaven, so great were the dangers and hardships of the journey.

> *Commentary:* Paul and Barnabas were taken for gods by the people of Lystra. They called Barnabas Zeus and Paul they thought to be Hermes because he was the chief speaker (Acts 14:8-18).

[35] While they were at this place one of the Fathers experienced the desire to find someone like those anchorites and Fathers who once lived in the great desert of Egypt, and he learned from what people were saying that about a mile and three quarters from the city a man was living as a solitary in a holy cell far from human contact.[16] Without

---

[13] GS 282[29] says that Estienne-Bonncrot, n. 234, gives the route from Verdun to Metz, but does not tell us what it is. In the main text, however, *GS* says that after Metz, "the companions mounted up the Moselle Valley and went past Pont-à-Mousson to Nancy, the capital of Lorraine, lying thirty-seven miles south of Metz. From here they continued their journey for two and one-half hours to Saint-Nicolas-du-Port on the bank of the Meurthe, a tributary of the Moselle."

[14] St. Nicholas of Myra, "good St. Nick" of American Christmases. *GS* 283 says that Joan of Arc visited the shrine in 1428.

[15] The Gothic church was begun in 1495, and was almost completed in 1536 when the companions visited it. *GS* 282. The structure has been completely restored at the end of the twentieth century thanks to the benefaction of a local lady who married a rich American and died childless. According to GS 283[37], the church today contains a commemorative window of Xavier. A pilgrim's guide written in 1893 maintains that Francis Xavier was miraculously cured there, confusing the story of Rodrigues about Francis in [5] above with his story about himself in [27] above. The confusion perseveres there today!

[16] Clearly this happened to Simão Rodrigues. *FN* 3:46[15].

telling the companions he immediately departs, and finds the place in ruins and uninhabited. About half way on the return a robust character suddenly appears squarely in his path. "You should know," he says, "that a very beautiful girl is waiting for you over there" (he pointed his finger at the place) "and is anxious to talk to you. Come with me and I'll take you to her." Then he stands in the middle of the road blocking his forward progress. "Look in whatever direction you want," he adds, "in no way are you going to avoid seeing this beautiful girl. So come and follow me." The next moment they were entangled in a wrestling match. Neither could throw the other to the ground and that huge rustic kept saying, "Me? You? You dare to fight with me?" The Father wanted very much to break the rustic's hold; he musters all his strength and with a mighty effort shakes him off. Thrown off, the man blocks the Father's way to the city. Then the Father, who was a novice in this kind of confrontation and little skilled in it, thinking to trick him by running quickly back to the shrine, heads full speed in that direction. Just as quickly his enemy follows him. The Father kneels before the altar for a moment and prays, leaves quickly by another door, and heads back for the city with the rustic following after. Then they went back to fighting in the same place as before, but breaking loose the Father flees as fast as he can with the man at his heels. He reaches the outskirts, and after running through most of the suburb, he sees the enemy still with him, keeping under the arcade of some buildings and with a finger raised to his nose, threatening him as if to say, "Believe you me, you're going to pay for this sometime." But Father believed that no one saw him when he was on the run, for he saw no one staring at him, and tired out from the fight and the run and covered with sweat even though it was extremely cold, he comes to the companions and says nothing about the incident.

Commentary: After his conversion Ignatius entertained the thought of joining the Carthusians (hermits who live in community). Early Jesuits were often tempted to spend long hours in prayer. Andrés de Oviedo asked Ignatius if he could spend seven years in prayer in a desert place; Francis Borgia lived in a hermitage part of the time in Spain; Simão Rodrigues would later live in a hermitage for some time after returning from Portugal in disgrace. St. Anthony, who provided much of the inspiration behind desert monasticism, endured violent sexual temptations. Is Simão telling this story to illustrate the temptation a Jesuit faces to live the hermit life with its concomitant sexual temptations? Is the story of the pimp who follows him an illustration of how constant can be that seductive call for a Jesuit to be a hermit? Does his failure to say anything about the incident to his companions reflect the reluctance of apostolic religious to talk about either the attraction of sex or the attraction of the hermit life? In the *Spiritual Exercises* Ignatius is very clear that the tempter urges secrecy and the tempted should reveal to someone wiser the hidden tactics of the evil one (*SpEx* 326).

[36] They left that city and after two or three days they all come to another part of Germany loyal to Emperor Charles V and King of Spain.[17] When the city fathers learned of their arrival, they summon the men. The French stay where they are and the Spaniards go to explain the reason for their journey. Asked who they were, they reply that they are Spaniards, that they have finished their studies in Paris, and are on their way to Italy to visit the shrine of Our Lady at Loreto, which they had certainly decided to do. They carefully gave this same account all through Germany. They were heard, and finally with auspiciously good luck they were ordered to move on. One of the officials, however, leaves the council and addresses the Fathers in Latin. He speaks contemptuously of the pilgrimage to Loreto, but they responded very well to his specious arguments which fell apart on their own.

[37] After the Fathers left there they spent over a month and a half before they came to Italy. Within the territory of heretics they endured bitter cold, unfamiliar with the languages and the roads (which as I

[17] Strasbourg, 312 miles from Paris (*GS* 284[44]), where *GS* 283 indicates that Bucer, the former Dominican monk, has taken over the spiritual leadership of the city from the bishop. *GS* 283[39] cites Caspar Hedio, *Ausserlessnen Chronick* (Strasburg, 1539) who gives two routes: (1) Luneville, Blamont, Saint-Quinn, Haslach, Mutzig, Molsheim, and (2) Wich (Vie) Tüse (Diuze), Münster, Sarwerd (Saarwerden), Lützelstein, Herrnstein, and Zabern (Saverne). *GS* notes that in 1520 the bishop of Strasbourg "had the 'Zabern path' cut through the cliffs and mountains, so that the ordinary route may have been from Saint-Nicholas-du-Port past Luneville, Blamont, Heming, Saarburg (Saarebourg), Lützelbourg (near Phalzbourg) and Zabern (Saverne) to Strasbourg (Martin Zeiler, *Itinerarium Germaniae* [Strasbourg, 1632], 229, and Sanson, 'Carte des Postes de France 1693,' *Nouvelle Introduction à la Géographice* [Paris, 1694])". In the main text *GS* chooses the third route, noting that at Saverne they enter German Alsace. According to the reconstructed journey it is now almost the end of November.

said, were blocked and hidden under a perpetual blanket of snow).
But God was their leader, and they had given themselves completely
to him. In him they placed their hope. By his grace and love they with
great joy and incredible happiness took on all difficulties, even the
struggle for life itself, and so they judged all things to be of less worth
than what they freely chose to undergo for God.

> *Commentary:* In this description Rodrigues hints that they lived
> out daily the Kingdom and the Two Standards of the Spiritual
> Exercises.

[38] Then after some days, worn out from the journey, weakened by
their struggles, almost exhausted by the severity of the cold and the
snow, they rested for about three or four days at Basle, a well-known
German city.[18] There people often came to them to dispute on matters
of faith. Our men boldly withstood those who came, refuted their
errors, and strenuously defended the truth of the holy Roman Church.
This unfortunate and unhappy city had strayed from orthodox belief,
and there was no evidence in it of divine worship except for sermons.
The church was superb, a beautiful edifice. In place of an altar and
images of the saints it had many wheels for making ropes. The heretics
of Basle were not accustomed at that time to bury their dead in the
church where the bodies of their parents lay buried, nor in the ceme-
tery nearby; but just as Catholic Christians dump the stinking cadav-
ers of dogs or other animals in a dung-pit outside the walls of the city,
so also they would bury their own dead in a field they had purchased,
no cross going before, no incense, no prayers for the dead (and it
would not have been a different ceremony if they had judged that they

---

[18] From Strasbourg to Basel, 78 miles, they had a choice: (1) the old Roman road:
Friesenheim, Markolsheim, Fessenheim, Ottmarsheim, Gross-Kembs, St. Eudwig or
(2): Matzenheim, Benfeld, Schlettstadt, Colmar, Ensisheim. *GS* 284[47]. *GS* 284 notes that
a statue of Our Lady from Catholic times greeted them at the Spalen gate of this
Protestant city, and says in n. 48 that it is still there today; furthermore, n.49 indicates
that a mandate of that time required that foreign Mass-priests not lodge in private
homes but in public inns. The present translator was there in the summer of 1965 with
a traveling seminar of priests and Protestant ministers and lay people. We were standing in front of a large church and a minister was regaling us with a tale about reformation days when Protestants were so opposed to "good works" that someone chipped
at a carving of St. Martin of Tours as a soldier giving half his cloak to a beggar so that
the beggar was turned into a tree stump. We were laughing heartily when someone
looked up and saw that we were standing in front of the church whose facade was both
graced and marred by this very carving! I do not know whether the companions saw
the same, but it certainly illustrates well the tension that existed between Catholics and
Protestants at that time.

were already burning in hell), no funeral ceremony whatever. There in the church lay Zwingli,[19] Œculampadius,[20] well known heretics, and a number of others, covered by a mound of earth, also Erasmus of Rotterdam.[21] At that time Karlstadt[22] was living in that city, a really deadly teacher of heresies, which for the most part were the aforementioned also. This is worth knowing, that heretics dwelling here and elsewhere, live miserably like fanatics and madmen. May God, who is always merciful and forgiving, have mercy on them one day.

[39] The companions knew no German,[23] and so they could not ask which direction they should go, with the result that they often wandered off course, up hill and down dale in snow more than knee-deep. But the Lord truly liberated them from these and all other dangers. It happened as well one time that when they made a mistake and wandered off course they came at night to a large village whose inhabitants were very close to abandoning the faith if they had not done so completely. They stopped at an inn where the whole night drinking, eating, singing, and dancing went on in honor of a priest, the local curate, who had taken a wife. That "good and worthy" priest, rejoicing in his bride, wore a huge sword at his side and kept flaunting it, brandishing it about jauntily.

[40] There is a town[24] about 15 miles before Constance whose spiritual shepherd had married a wife and was supporting a numerous flock of children. He was well versed in a deadly heretical sect, but

---

[19] Rodrigues is mistaken. Zwingli was killed in a battle at Kappel 11 October 1531 warring against Catholics. His body was cut to pieces and thrown into a fire. *FN* 3:48[17].

[20] Johann Œcolampadius (1482-1531). *FN* 3:48[18]. His theological position was between Luther, Zwingli, and Calvin. The stone on his sepulcher was not laid until 1542. *GS* 286[64].

[21] Erasmus (1466-1536) died at Basel a few months before the companions passed through there. *FN* 3:48[19]. "The original marker placed on Erasmus's tomb in 1537 has disappeared. In 1928 the present stone with an inscription dating from 1538 was transferred along with the tomb itself to the first pillar of the choir in the Schaler chapel." *GS* 286[65].

[22] Andreas Rudolf Bodenstein, born about 1480, called Karlstadt after the city of his birth. He left the Catholic faith at Wittenberg in 1522, went to Basle in 1534, and died there about 1541. *FN* 3:49[20].

[23] *GS* 289: "still less the guttural Alemannic dialect of this region."

[24] Weinfelden. *GS* 289[79]: "Instead of continuing straight ahead after crossing the Thur at Märstetten, the travelers followed the course of the river east to Weinfelden."

obviously of average intelligence.[25] Learning of the Fathers' arrival, he gathers together six or seven of the leading citizens and comes to them at night to argue against the Catholic faith, all tired out as they were from the journey. So much time was spent disputing that after some hours the curate said, "'Look, it's a rainy night, and the setting stars suggest it's time for supper (*caenam*).'[26] Now tomorrow [if I may use his own words] I absolutely want you to go to my house and see my books (*libros*) and my children (*liberos*). Let us eat, therefore, and after eating let us continue the contest." His counsel prevailed. "But," they say, "let us all sit together at the same table." "Indeed not," reply the Fathers. "Are we to be forced to eat with heretics, men separated from the bosom of the Church? That will never be; we will not ever do that." Zeal for the faith consumed them to that extent.[27] The priest smiled. He and his group used one table, the Fathers another. After dinner the dispute resumed so vigorously and efficaciously on the part of one Father[28] who stung the heretic so effectively that the cleric said, after being pushed into a corner, "I'm all through." "Why, then," added another Father, "do you embrace a sect you cannot defend?" Feigning that he was offended by this response, he rises in a fury and threatening to put the Fathers in chains, says, "Shall I teach you tomorrow in jail whether I know how to defend my sect or not?" Then barking out

[25] GS 290[81]: "Weinfelden was reformed in 1536. There was no Catholic priest in the town at this time since Ulrich Vor, the former pastor, had become an Evangelical in 1528. In 1536 the Protestant minister was Martin Motteli, who had probably been born in Weinfelden. He had studied Scripture and had been educated in the teaching of the Reformation. The justice Hans Ulrich of Sax deemed it necessary to warn him about this. He died in 1576, probably in Weinfelden."

[26] A quote from Virgil's *Aeneid*, Book II, verses 8-9, except that in the *Aeneid* it is time for sleep (*somnos*). FN 3:50[23].

[27] The companions missed a golden opportunity here, a chance to get to know their adversaries in a non-combative context. A few years later, Peter Faber, who acquired more experience than the others in "dealing with heretics," wrote to Diego Laínez that one who wants to succeed with heretics should look upon them with love and close his mind to anything that would tend to lessen his affection for them. He should try to gain their good will so that they in turn will love him. Be friendly; stress the points of agreement and avoid disagreements. Appeal primarily to the affections rather than the intellect: speak on holiness of life, the practice of virtue, whatever stirs toward moral reawakening, rather than on pronouncements of authority designed to confound them. Letter of 7 March 1546, MF 399-402, E.T. *The Spiritual Writings of Pierre Favre* (St. Louis: Institute of Jesuit Sources, 1966) 379-81; see extracts in William V. Bangert, S.J., *To the Other Towns: a Life of Blessed Peter Favre, First Companion of St. Ignatius* (Westminster, Md.: Newman Press, 1959) 253-56.

[28] Laínez, according to Orlandini's history of the Society, 1. I, 113. See [L34].

something in German,[29] he left the inn. The companions, happy for the opportunity to suffer and die in defense of the Catholic faith, regretted only the possibility of being separated from one another. At night therefore they all pour out prayers to God. In the morning at daybreak a man comes in, tall, well formed, handsome, about thirty to judge from his appearance. He looks at the Fathers with a smile and says in German, "Follow me. I'll show you the way." Suddenly all of them follow him without an objection; they trust him; they believe him. He brings them outside the town and leads them by crossroads for about seven miles and finally indicates the royal highway. While walking he often looked at the companions and smiled gently, his face suffused with joy; he told them to be of good heart and not to fear deceit or danger of any sort. Part of this route looked to be more difficult, but with no snow all around it was found to be very easy. One of the companions began to watch the terrain, looking one way and then another: this was no well-traveled road, and examining the terrain more carefully, there was no sign of the royal highway or any crossroad. Astonished, therefore, at the novelty of seeing that this more difficult stretch had no snow and everywhere else was covered, he kept saying to himself, "Truly, who is this man who is familiar with the most unknown roads?" But since God, who providentially created the universe, was preserving the companions for greater things, he took particular care that they did not perish in that town, for by virtue of his own guide he led them back to the royal highway where there were traces of passing travelers. But finally their gracious and friendly guide pointed out to the companions the way they should go, and with a gentle and modest smile, grave but cheerful, he quietly sent them on their way.[30] With his departure the companions experienced themselves left all alone, abandoned and wholly without protection.

> *Commentary:* Whatever happened here, Simão makes it clear
> that as far as he was concerned either Jesus or an angel of the

[29] That is, in the Alemannic dialect. *GS* 290[88] suggests "an Alemannic slang expression such as 'Chaibepfaffe' or 'Saupfaffechaibe.'" The present translator tried to find an equivalent in German: if *chaibe* is related to *schäbig* in German, the first expression could be: "Shabby priest!" and the second could be "Sau" (sow/filthy creature) Pfaffe (priest) chaibe (shabby) = "Dirty, unkempt priest!" or the equivalent.

[30] *GS* 291[89]: "The man was probably a Catholic; there were still Catholic families in Weinfelden in 1536. It lay in the religiously neutral canton of Thurgau." This person led the companions by way of Mt. Otten (671 m., 2,180 ft.) to the highway going from Frauenfeld to Constance. *FN* 3:52[25]; *GS* 291[90]. Is Schurhammer missing Simão's story of God's work in the companions'? Is not Simão having a religious experience?

Lord guided them out of the town and up the mountain side. Like Jesus or the angel on Easter morning the young man appears at daybreak, not quite recognizable (for he talks German). "Follow me," he says, just as Jesus had called his apostles, and in the same manner they follow him with complete trust. He leads them the way the angel led Peter out of the jail, passing without difficulty one obstacle after another (Acts 12:6-11). The companions are in grave difficulties, as were the apostles during the storm at sea, and Simão asks a question similar to that found in Luke 8:25, "Who then is this, that he commands even the winds and the water, and they obey him?" Finally, he shows them the way. Does Simão recognize the man as *being* the way? Certainly he sees the event as providential. The young man, or one somewhat like him, will appear in the story again [56].

[41] On that day they came to Constance which had at that time already defected from the Catholic faith by common consent. Nevertheless, there was a church outside the city near the walls where Mass[31] was allowed as long as those who heard Mass paid a price—some sort of coin more or less equivalent to a denarius.[32] They left there and, after enduring severe cold and various trials, the Fathers directed their way to a town whose name I do not recall.[33] About a mile before arriving there they suddenly came upon a hospital for those who suffered from a noisome and contagious eczema.[34] An old woman, seeing the men with rosaries hanging around their necks and intuiting that they were Catholic, runs up to them, raises her eyes to

[31] The chapel of the monastery of the Canons Regular of St. Augustine, called Kreutzlingen after a bishop of Constance (1334-44). *FN* 3:53[26]. GS 291[95]: "It stood near the city gate until 1633 . . . The north wall of the present inn, 'Zum Schäpfle,' seems originally to have been the south wall of the monastery. . . . The monastery burned down in 1499, but was rebuilt in 1502."

[32] *GS* 292[96]: "This probably refers to the small fee for confession which was then customary (Böhmer 196)."

[33] Apparently Lindau. *FN* 3:53[27]. After thorough research and changing his earlier opinion, *GS* 292[98] routes them from Constance "six miles straight across the north arm of the lake to Meersburg. From here it was still twenty-five miles to Lindau, the last Protestant city" (n. 99).

[34] *GS* 293[101]: "He means the infirmary for poor lepers in Aeschach, less than a mile north of Lindau, located on the site now occupied by the parish house of Aeschach. The adjoining meadow, known as 'Der Siechenbrühl' [infirmary meadow] perpetuates the site. The chapel dedicated to St. Gangolf, which was demolished in 1901, belonged to it."

heaven, spreads out her arms in the form of a cross, and crying out in German, kisses the rosaries. The Fathers did not know what she was saying, but from her pantomime they judged she was a Catholic. By her gestures and other gesticulations, she tells the Fathers to wait. She quickly runs into the hospital and returns immediately with a lap full of rosaries, arms, legs, and heads of statues of saints which the heretics had criminally violated. The companions kneel on the ground, which was covered with snow, prostrate themselves and piously kiss the bits of the statues of the saints. The woman rejoices, exults, waves her arms, and unable to contain her joy heads for the city together with the Fathers. They hardly get through the gate and she starts screaming. With loud cries she scolds the heretics (as we learned later after someone translated the words). "Look! Look!" she said, "Look, you scoundrels, you deceitful wretches, look, you complete frauds, look at these Christian men! Didn't you tell me, you deceivers, that all mortal beings had sworn fealty to the pestilential errors of the heretics? You lie, you lie openly, you criminals. It's false. Are you trying to deceive me? You'll never deceive me. I know you inside out." Then we found out that this old woman could not ever be persuaded by threats or bribes to embrace an heretical sect. Therefore, after being driven from the city, she had been living in that hospital with the sick. Afterwards one of the heretics often insisted that she far surpassed other women in madness and stubbornness, and that even if the whole world by common consent would assent to the truth of the faith (for that is what they called their errors), this stubborn woman will cling to her own opinion and defend her own position regardless.[35] Here the Fathers repeatedly agreed to the usual contest with the heretics. When they would cite some passages from holy Scripture, the heretics responded that was not the way it was. Then they would open their Bibles which Martin Luther had translated from Latin into German and would examine the passage; for in these Bibles almost all the passages that could clearly show up their errors were full of inaccuracies or completely expunged.

---

[35] According to *GS* 293[102] a poor leper named Mrs. Anna Mürglin was allowed to live with the poor sick in the hospital for incurables at Lindau. She lost this benefit for misbehaving but later was reinstated because she promised to improve and her sufferings were so far advanced she could not use the leper's clapper to warn other people when begging. *GS* wonders if this is the woman in Simão's story and whether her misbehavior was her stubborn adherence to the old faith.

These are the remarks I have to make about the pilgrimage through Germany. Although the Fathers were exhausted by many other trials and dangers, I shall pass over them in silence lest I take too much time, and I shall briefly narrate what happened to them after they came to Venice.[36]

[36] *GS* 294, n. 104: two possibilities (1) northern route along the old Roman road to Kempten, Füssen, Reutte, Lermoos, and the Fern pass; (2) southern route opened in 1218, through Bregenz, Feldkirch and the Arlberg, passing through Catholic territory, the more likely path since no further mention is made of contacts with Protestants. *GS* 294-95: "Leaving Lake Constance behind them, they continued south up the broad valley of the Rhine. After a day's walk they arrived at the old city of Feldkirch. From here their road went east through a wild gorge into the broad valley of the Ill, flanked by lofty Alpine mountains, to Bludenz, and then through the narrow valley of the Kloster over the Arlberg pass to Landeck. Here there was a fork in the road, one branch going east down the valley of the Inn past Innsbruck to the Brenner pass, and the other going south up the same valley over the Finstermünz pass in the valley of the Etsche to Meran. Near Bolzano the two routes again converged. Here, in the midst of the beautiful snows of the Tyrolese Alps, the travelers celebrated Christmas. From Bolzano they went south to Trent, where German was no longer spoken but Italian instead. From here they took the direct road for Venice, which skirted the yawning abysses of the dangerous Horni Blatna pass in the wild and romantic Val Sugana. Beyond Primolano the lofty, sheer rock cliffs came close together, leaving at times hardly enough space for the mule track and tumbling brook. At Brassano they passed from the mountain into the fruitful Venetian plain. A two days' walk brought them from here past Castelfranco and Mestre to the Adriatic Sea. On January 8, two days after the feast of the Epiphany, the companions, in good health and cheerful spirits, entered the city of the Lagoons."

CHAPTER FOUR: Venice . . . Rome, 1537

[42] They came therefore to Venice and there with great joy they found Ignatius waiting for them.[1] Without any delay they began to discuss what they should do until the time came to board ship for Jerusalem (for they still had to wait about half a year). They finally decided that they would spend part of the time serving the poor in the hospitals, part on the journey they would make sooner or later to ask for the blessing of the sovereign pontiff. For the companions were convinced that with his blessing their affairs would prosper more under the care and providence of God Almighty. They therefore choose two hospitals to work in with their poor and sick (one called Sts. John and Paul and the other the Incurables)[2] divided into two groups.[3] Sometimes Ignatius, who was living in another house,[4] visited them at work, and sometimes they visited him. In the hospitals they waited on the indigent, made the beds, swept the house, cleaned

---

[1] Ignatius was studying theology and living at La Trinità, a priory of the Teutonic Order. The prior was Monsignor Andrea Lippomani. He had helped Ignatius before and after his pilgrimage to the Holy Land. The priory was situated on the south bank of the Grand Canal shortly before one came to St. Mark's Square, opposite the Contarini palace between the Customs Office on the farthest point of the Dorsoduro peninsula and the abbey church of St. Gregory. The church was ornate, had a beautiful garden with a well at the center. GS 299. While waiting for his companions Ignatius had picked up a new companion, Diego Hozes, a priest from Malaga in Spain, directing him through the Exercises, and Hozes had committed himself to the pilgrimage and work of the other companions. GS 292. Two fathers who made the Spiritual Exercises under Ignatius's direction at that time were Pier Contarini, a distant relative of Cardinal Gasparo Contarini, and Gasparo de Dotti (see below [87]). Pier Contarini was one of the procurators of the hospital for incurables and its main support. GS 304.

[2] Known as Zattere allo Spirito Santo 423, the present Distretto Militare. GS 306[90].

[3] Five of them ministered in each hospital, in the hospital of Sts. John and Paul: two besides Hozes, Rodrigues and apparently Salmerón, who is said to have had a close relationship with Gasparo di Dotti, who lived in the adjoining monastery; in the hospital for the Incurables: Faber, Xavier, Laínez, along with two other companions. Faber and Hozes heard confessions. FN 3:57[2]. GS 305[85].

[4] In a letter of 12 February 1536 to Diego Caçador, archdeacon of Barcelona, Ignatius writes: "I enjoy the companionship and home of a very good and devout man, so that nothing in these parts could suit my purposes better." EI 1:94. Andrea Lippomani received him as guest . . . and there he continued his study of theology. FN 3:57[3]. The same letter reveals his desire to "preach in poverty" wherever God sends him without the "cumbersome comforts" of his time in study. EI 1:96.

out whatever was soiled, washed the pots of the poor who were sick, carried away the bodies of the dead honorably prepared for burial, dug their graves and buried them in a religious manner. Day and night they were present to everyone with such care, fervor, joy and happiness that all those living in the hospitals were greatly astounded. Rumors even spread throughout the city, and noblemen and important personages talked about it. They often came to the hospitals to see for themselves, conceiving a high opinion of their sanctity and learning.

> *Commentary:* In tales of chivalry, knightly exploits were not limited to slaying dragons and giants but extended to rescuing the weak and the poor. The "incurables" were those suffering from syphilis, a repulsive disease in which the body was covered with sores exuding pus with a repugnant stench. That the actions of the companions were heroic is clear from the fact that people came to witness what they were doing.

[43] One thing I would not wish is to be buried in silence. The Fathers spent time not only in higher studies and sweating hard at work. They also habitually took great care to talk to the poor about matters of God and also about their salvation when necessary.

> *Commentary:* The *Formula of the Institute* speaks not only of the propagation of the faith but first of all of "the progress of souls in Christian life and doctrine," and also of "the instruction in Christianity of children and the uninitiated." Many of the poor and of the sick were profoundly ignorant of their faith.

[44] While the Fathers were doing these things, each one tried, in as manly a way as he could, to overcome the movements of repugnance stirred within them from the stench of the place, the filth, and the sight of the horrible wounds.[5] I could go on freely here for there is a lot of

---

[5] Rodrigues refers to the disease as leprosy. GS 308 describes the situation: "This work in the hospital required a very great deal of self-conquest on the part of the nurses. The 'French disease' began with a fever. Then the whole body was covered with ugly and repulsive sores two fingers wide. These were round and raised above the surrounding surface of the skin, and were larger and worse than those of measles. They were often full of pus and exuded an evil smell that lasted for several months. They were so repulsive that frequently even the physicians fled away in disgust. The rash spread over the whole body, but especially on the face, right up to the eyes. The sores often took the shape of thick, hard, irregular crusts of a dark green color extending also

ground to cover, but not to be too long, I shall try to stay within the proposed bounds of brevity, content with recalling one or other event. In the hospital for incurables a leper, or a person with something resembling leprosy, completely covered with some kind of contagious eczema, calls out to one of the Fathers,[6] "You there, please scratch my back." The Father diligently undertook the task, but in the middle of scratching, overcome by disgust and almost ready to throw up, he begins to fear that he might catch some infectious disease. But because he has a greater desire to overcome his feelings than to worry about the future, he scrapes the diseased matter with his fingers, then puts them in his mouth, licks them, and sucks them. The next day he tells the story to his companion and says, smiling, "I dreamt last night that the leprosy of a sick man had infected my throat and that I had tried in vain to get rid of it by coughing and spitting." He had made a bonafide effort to overcome himself, and what Christ our Lord said was fulfilled in him, "And if they drink anything deadly, no harm will come to them" [Mk. 16:18].

[45] On top of that, in the middle of the night, the infirmarian did not want to admit another poor person infected with leprosy into the hospital of Sts. John and Paul, saying there was no empty bed. The beggar insisted anyway and he refused him again. One of the companions,[7] however, moved by compassion, begs the infirmarian to admit him. "I shall provide a bed and a room," he says. He is admitted and the companion shares his bed with the beggar. The next day in the morning, the poor man was nowhere in the hospital and the Father arose completely covered with leprosy. Even so, he was not sad, but

to the hands and feet, giving one the appearance of a leper. But the sores were worse than those of lepers because of their unbearable stench, which betrayed the nature of the disease. Besides this, the sick were afflicted with headaches which at times did not allow them to sleep for forty, sixty, or even a hundred days. The victims as a consequence cried out continuously and collapsed under their pains. They were also subject to attacks of fever and deep moral and physical depression. The sores lasted as a rule for a year, but frequently longer. They then disappeared but would suddenly return with even greater virulence. A kind of cancerous rot then set in and began to eat away one member after the other: nose, lips, gums, eyes, and so forth. The disease was regarded as being extremely contagious and incurable."

[6] Francis Xavier, according to [L35]. FN 3:58[4]. GS 309[109] says that later a portrait of Xavier was placed there with an inscription indicating that Xavier had celebrated Mass there (he was not yet ordained) and had cured a sick man (which the text does not suggest).

[7] Simão Rodrigues. FN 3:59[6].

joyfully said to the others, "It's nothing, brothers, it's nothing." He was very sad, however, for their sakes, but the next day he rose from his bed completely healthy; the leprosy had disappeared as though he had never been touched by this noxious disease.

[46] In the hospital for incurables at that time, out of devotion women used to prepare food for the sick, both women and men. Whenever the Fathers entered the kitchen to bring food to some sick person, one of the women always glared at them grimly and screamed insults at them shamelessly. So it came about that one of the companions said to another, "I don't know who this woman is; every time I go into the kitchen she rants at me, and I don't know what she is grumbling about." The other replied, "She is also angry with me. I think she is possessed by the devil, for when I happened to be present, she spoke very clearly to the others saying, 'You seem to be totally unaware of who these people are. They are outstanding and learned men. I have tried as best I could to keep them out of here, but I have gotten nowhere.'" The Father noted the words and immediately concluded she was besieged by the devil. When he went into the kitchen the next time, she screamed loudly at him. When he tried to soothe her with quiet words, she ran off ready to throw herself into the fire, but another woman who was there prevented her from doing what she wanted to do. Then knowing for sure that she was under the power of the devil, he takes her hand and says to the other women, "Let her be." But the possessed woman, with the fireplace at her back, says, "If you don't let me go, I'll throw myself into the fire." He had scarcely let go when she did a back flip turning around on the spot, so that since the Father had completely let go of her, she almost fell into the fire head first. Regaining her balance, she filled the place with loud cries so that the women were terrified. Many people who were aroused by the cries came running, along with the priest who was the chaplain for the hospital. The priest immediately brings the wild woman into the church and in God's name according to the rite of the Church he orders the evil spirit to leave her body. Ordered to recite the Creed, she uttered some words brokenly, jumping from one word to another and leaving some out. When she finally came to the words, "from thence he shall come to judge the living and the dead," the evil spirit groaned horribly and cried out, "Alas! What shall I do on that fearful day!" And the woman stood there for a bit like someone lifeless and dead. I could recount much more about that demon, but there is no

need to say any more than is helpful.

> *Commentary:* This story has a touch of Acts 16:16ff, where Paul and Silas and Luke encounter "a slave-girl who had the power of divination and brought her owners a great deal of money by fortune-telling. While she followed Paul and us, she would cry out, 'These men are slaves of the Most High God, who proclaim to you a way of salvation.'"

[47]   Although it may perhaps seem foreign to my purpose, one should be aware nevertheless that Italy, at the time of the Fathers' arrival there, was unfamiliar with frequenting the sacraments of the Eucharist and the confession of sins. So true this was that if someone went to confession and communion once a week everybody talked about it and wrote to their friends in other places as though something new and unusual had happened. Besides, at this time the Blessed Sacrament of Christ's Body was brought to the sick without pomp, without a large retinue, so that it was necessary for God to work a miracle and for men to be taught by donkeys. "Ask the beasts, and they will teach you" [Job 12:7]. This is what happened. A priest, bringing the heavenly bread to a sick man living outside the city, came across a pack of donkeys in a field. The donkeys run up to the approaching curate, and, as though they were rational creatures, they throw themselves on the ground on their knees on both sides of the road. The priest, along with a boy who was his only companion, awed by the unheard-of reverence shown by the animals toward the most holy sacrament, walks between the rows of donkeys. They all rise in the same order in which they had been kneeling and follow the priest who goes along as though leading a procession. While they were with the sick man, astonished at the miracle, they kept wondering what it portended. The priest and his attendant as well, overcome by awe, kept telling the story. And so the priest, after refreshing the sick man with the most sacred Body of Christ, went out and bestowed a blessing on all those standing outside by the doors. After receiving it, the donkeys also, who seemed to be expecting it, returned happily to their usual grazing spot prancing with joy. The event was duly noted in the public records after many witnesses had been very carefully interrogated. When the Fathers came to Venice, the story was being told publicly by preachers in their sermons. And that is the origin of that society, the Confraternity of the Most Holy Sacrament of the Eucharist. This

extraordinary miracle took place in the Republic of Venice, in the parish of a certain town called, if I am not mistaken, Villa Nova, near Astiano,[8] the estate of our college in Padua. And since I was there and took considerable effort that the truth of the event might come to light, I have dared to insert its little story here.

> *Commentary:* Although the event described is not a part of the companions' pilgrimage and may be open to challenge as more imagination than fact, their devotion to the Blessed Sacrament is very much a part of their pilgrimage, a fact that cannot be challenged.

[48]   The Fathers were in the hospitals for two and a half months. Then, leaving Ignatius in Venice, they set out for Rome.[9] For the first time they made the journey in poverty, living on alms begged from door to door, and sleeping sometimes in hospitals, at other times in haylofts, and sometimes in cattle-sheds, weary, with clothes, shoes and leggings soaking wet, yet no one got sick (which truly amazes me). In hospitals they would teach the needy Christian doctrine and prayers the poor did not know. They were so committed to poverty and careful about it that they would not depart a hair's breadth from it. They collected only as much food as they judged enough for the present moment and kept nothing in reserve for later. With people they happened to meet they engaged quietly and effectively in spiritual conversation, and they spent a good part of the trip doing this and reciting litanies and chanting the psalms of David. When some people thought about this and noticed the difficult way of life they followed, and considered their holy conversation and their frequent comments on divine things, they decided that they were men who had taken part in the recent sack of Rome and therefore were imposing difficult penances on themselves and were going to Rome to beg absolution from the Roman Pontiff.

---

[8] The Latin and Portuguese have *Hastiano*; a German translation has *Astiano*. There seems to be a town called "Ostiano" not far from Padua that has some relation to the Gonzaga family, but its exact distance from Padua is uncertain. "Hastiano" or "Astiano" could simply be the name of the estate, or perhaps "estate" should be "general area."

[9] *GS* 309 says that Hozes joined them for the pilgrimage to Loreto and Rome, as did Antonio Arias, a priest, and Miguel Landívar, Xavier's former servant in Paris.

[49]   Leaving Venice[10] they started for Ancona on the shore of the Adriatic Sea.[11] On this trip the companions spent two or three days with almost no food (and there was no place until Ravenna where alms could be gathered).[12] Meanwhile it happened that, because of the lack of food and the difficulties of the road, they became so weak that they could go no farther nor could they go back.[13] And so, with no hope in any human source of consolation, they vigorously commended themselves to God (the only remedy left them). In these difficulties it was clear that each one was more affected by the others' problems and more deeply moved by the others' afflictions and difficulties than by their own. Sometimes they were so weak that out of weariness some would lie down on the ground and others would sit down on the earth. One privately said to another who had fasted a lot in Venice, "Do you remember, Father," he says, "our former poverty in Venice, where this kind of toil didn't even cross our minds, and we both cheated ourselves of the bread we needed to keep our bodies going?" Then without doubting that he was understood, he immediately adds, "I shall try hard not to have that happen again. I promise that I shall never again not take when I can enough bread to sustain life and other demanding labors." The Father said this out of compassion for the others who were weak and feeble and deprived of human resources, for he added, "If I had any of the strength I used to have, if I still had the energy that faded away on account of the fasts we both maintained, not getting enough to eat to sustain ourselves, I would go around the countryside to beg help in meeting the needs of the Fathers and bring back some sort of relief for them." But finally their strength for going on returned providentially, and they continued the journey,

[10] As Rodrigues indicates a little further below, after two or three days' journey the companions arrived in Ravenna on Passion Sunday, 18 March. Therefore they can be said to have left Venice on 15 or 16 March. The distance was 112 km: 22 km. to Chioggia, and 90 km. to Ravenna. They spent two nights, one, it seems, in a place called Le Fornaci, the other in the town of Magnavacca. It was a very difficult journey according to Rodrigues, Laínez and others, both because it was almost uninhabited so that food was hard to find, and because the mouth of the Po River was flooded. *FN* 3:64[11]. They may have taken a ship from Venice to Choggia. *GS* 311[2, 6-8.] "The appearance of the Po Delta has changed greatly in the course of time" *GS* 312[10].

[11] This is the so-called "Via Romea," described by Bartholomew Fontana who traveled it in 1538. *FN* 3:65[12].

[12] Somewhere along the journey they could see the church tower of the abbey of Pomposa. *GS* 314, and 314[24].

[13] Peter Ribadeneira and Jerome Doménech endured similar difficulties on the same journey in 1543. *FN* 3:65[13].

although only slightly refreshed by food.[14]

[50] Then they came upon a river that had risen so high from continual downpours that it flooded a mile or so beyond the stream bed. By begging that day they picked up only two small loaves, of which one or the other provided a small bite for each one since they had certainly not dined on anything more sumptuous the day before. When the Fathers had come to the bank of the river, they ask the ferryman to take them across. The ferryman shakes his head saying that in no way can it be done. The companions, in terrible straits for lack of food and the need to cross the river, press the ferryman as much as they can to take them across. Worn down by their begging, he brings them to a rise on another part of the bank, pointing out the twists and turns they need to follow. They cover two thirds of a mile or so with the water sometimes up to their waist, sometimes up to their chest. Coming out of that flood at last, they come upon a pine forest nearby.[15] Suddenly, driven by hunger, they fall on the pine cones, break them open and eat the nuts. A lot of work, not much food, a lot of time spent; so it was clear to all that they had to press on. These events took place on Passion Sunday;[16] on this day one of the Fathers was cured whose foot had been infected with an itch for a long time.[17] Finally, at night, wet, weary, and worn out with hunger, they were admitted into a hospice.

[14] GS 315[26] locates this incident on the stretch between Goro and Volano. The town of Goro followed the movement of the delta and at present is 6 miles southeast of Mesola and 4 miles from Volano. GS 314[22]. GS 315 suggests they were able to get food at the Watchtower of Volano (Torre di Volano).

[15] Pineta di San Vitale, still standing today. FN 3:67[15]. It runs east of the Via Romea from north to south and is not to be confused with the Pineta di Classe, near Sant'Apollinare south of Ravenna, made famous by Dante. GS317[43].

[16] 18 March. FN 3:68[16]. Earlier in the day they had crossed another river by ferry. After saying Mass Hozes asked from the people in attendance an alms to pay the ferry, unaware that this was contrary to the custom of the companions, and they gave him only 2 quatrines. When the companions reached the river people gave them 14 or 15 quatrines without being asked, precisely what they needed. They gave the 2 quatrines to Hozes saying, "Take your quatrines, for you know that God has no need for the quatrines you asked for at Mass." Then they crossed the river and a man shared his meal with them [L38]. Later in the day came this second flooded river. At another river when they had no money a man said, "I see you are reluctant to change your escudos, so I'll pay for you" [L38].

[17] John Codure [L37]. FN 3:68[17].

[51] It further came to pass that when three of the companions came
to the same hospice[18] they were shown a bed that was dirty and much-
used; it sheets were damp, bloody, and very spotted. In spite of this
one of them was not afraid to crawl in even with nothing on, and a second one at least dressed. The third,[19] deterred by the squalor, found
rest elsewhere. Thinking about it later, he was very sorry that he had
been overcome in this battle. He longed for an occasion to be offered
to him where he could repair what he ascribed to the weakness, indul-
gence, and softness of his body. God fulfilled his desire. For when he
came with another companion to a hospital in a certain area,[20] a
woman who was in charge of the hospital told him she had no bed
except for one in which a sick man had been lying who that day had
departed from this life with phthiriasis.[21] She said the sheets were
clean, however, and the sick man had not lain on them while alive.
They had been placed there for his dead body out of reverence for the
cross and the priests who had come to the hospital to commend the
body of the dead man to God and to bury it. In this matter the woman
did not deceive the Fathers, for they were still sprinkled with holy
water and covered with large lice which the disease normally pro-
duced. The Father therefore, who wanted to claim a victory after his
initial defeat, seizes the opportunity and throws himself undressed on
the sheets. At once the lice rush upon him, sting him all night long,
annoy the naked man and feed on him so harshly that they make him
perspire. But the Father conquered himself, overcame and conquered
himself gloriously. His companion, however, lay down in the same
place fully clothed.

[52] And so they came to Ravenna. After that they went on in twos
and threes since it was not possible in all these places to get enough
for so many from alms. Besides, it was the rainy season, and the rivers
were inundated by frequent rains. In addition, while the ferrymen

---

[18] *Ospedale degli infermi,* now the *Scuola Normale Femminile* on the street called
Girotto Guaccimanni, n. 3. *FN*3:68[18]. According to a local tradition "the two corner
windows in the upper story facing the Via Marco Dente . . . had been Xavier's room."
GS 318[49].

[19] Rodrigues. *FN* 3:69[19].

[20] *GS* 326[105] thinks this place might be Muccia, a village between Tolentino and
Foligno, a normal place to stop after they left Loreto for Rome.

[21] A morbid condition of the body in which lice multiply excessively, causing
extreme irritation. *OED* 801c.

were refusing to take the companions across without the fare they lacked, they often gave them no little trouble, and so on occasion they were forced to pay the price of passage sometimes with writing materials and sometimes with a linen doublet.[22]   At Ravenna therefore while one of the Fathers[23] was gathering money to hire a boat in which he might be carried to a neighboring part along with two companions, he by chance came upon a building with which he was completely unfamiliar.[24] There he begs for alms on the steps of a very long flight of stairs. Ordered to come up higher, he goes up. There he confronts three elegantly beautiful girls, morally dissolute and with no sense of shame. Recognizing from their words and unbounded license that they had little modesty, he went back down faster than he had come up. The girls immediately call the man, urge him not to go away. In no way, however, does he slow down, and now at almost the bottom in a little niche on the far side of the staircase he begins to preach with great zeal as the Spirit moved him. The girls come down to see the preacher better. They were beginning to show signs of repentance, especially one of them who was shedding an abundance of tears, when behold a monk shows up unexpectedly at an entrance, all by himself, without a companion, wearing the habit of an Augustinian friar, glum, with enflamed and bloodshot eyes, chipped and broken teeth and some almost worn away. Then all on fire with rage he addresses the Father in Spanish as though this was his personal business, "Ho, there, Master," he says, "Come on down from there, let the women go. What have you got to do with them? Are you determined to bring them to a healthier way of life? You will fail, they are certainly not going to come to their senses. Come on, come on, let them go. Why waste your time and energy? Send them away and come on down." The Father, as he was angry, does not change his approach. But the girl who had begun to cry, as though moved by God, says to the Father, "Miserable and unhappy me! What hope is left for my salvation? None at all unless I accompany you to Rome. There with your help, I might find a better way of living." The Father urges her to move and adopt a better way of living, but points out that going to Rome

---

[22] *GS* 313[14] suggests the writing materials went to cross the Brenta, and the doublet to cross the Etsch.

[23] Rodrigues, obviously.

[24] "The harbor of Ravenna, which has been completely silted up since 1736, lay near the church of Santa Maria in Porto Fuori on the Fiumi Uniti two miles southeast of the Porta Nuova" *GS* 319[51].

with his group would be inappropriate. Then he leaves the women and addresses the monk who was listening to all this with gloomy eyebrow raised. "May God bless you," he says, "Where did you come from all by yourself, and where are you going?" "From Rome," he replies, "and I'm going to Venice." Without saying much, he left, and as though he was going about some business, he started walking along a broad street like a market-place that extended to the river's shore where the rowers get into the boats. He moved briskly now this way, now that way. He went back and forth, more like a customs official worried that his profit or gain was going to be snatched from him surreptitiously on the spot rather than like a religious monk. The Father could not help but be greatly amazed at him as he watched him turning aimlessly back and forth all over the place. When, therefore, he wanted to board the skiff along with his companions, behold the weeping girl is there. "I'm going with you," she says. The Father explains to the companions who did not know what had happened, while lots of people who knew what was going on gathered around on the bank of the river and were talking to one another about it. But when the Fathers said to her as she tried to get on board that they would not go with her, the ferryman finally prevented her and they set sail, while the girl keeps on weeping bitterly as they sail away.

> *Commentary:* This scene seems like a morality play. Simão is in unfamiliar territory; he hears a call to come up higher reflective of Jesus's parable in Luke 14:10, and in responding finds himself face to face with three alluring prostitutes. Fleeing from them, he begins to preach, and they follow. A monk who seems to be a caricature of Luther enters the scene and interrupts his preaching. The girls are inclined toward repentance, especially one of them, a sort of Magdalen figure with all her tears, and wants to come with them, but the companions decree/discern that her presence in their company is inappropriate. The story seems to reflect the work that Ignatius eventually did in Rome in establishing the House of Martha for repentant prostitutes.

[53] In a port to which the Fathers sailed after they left Ravenna, they learned from listening to others that they had more rivers to cross between there and Ancona. Besides, since it was raining all the time it seemed they would have to take another skiff. And so they boarded it without any food, without any drink, indeed without any money to pay the fare to the ferryman. Arriving at Ancona after a whole day

and an entire night, they tell the captain, who is demanding payment, that they do not have so much as a farthing. The ferryman, angry as can be, refuses to let them disembark; he even takes an oath that he will not let them leave the ship. Even so the companions ask the man to allow one of the Fathers to leave who might pick up something to satisfy him by begging. He finally accedes to this request. The companion, since he was not yet ordained and did not have to recite the divine office, goes to a bookseller and sells him his breviary on the condition that if he returns the money within a specified amount of time, the bookseller will also return the breviary immediately (for the bookseller had bought the book for an unfair price). Then he quickly returns to the companions after making the deal, they all head for the hospice together where two of the others were already who had come a little earlier. All of them (except for one who was left in the hospice for the poor) scatter throughout the streets of the city and beg alms from door to door.

[54] Here one of the companions,[25] picking up an alms, saw another companion in the market-place, barefoot, his clothes pulled up to his knees, begging among the women who were selling their wares, picking up a radish from one, an apple from another, and similar things from others, accepting them with the greatest humility. Then when he began to consider this man's poverty and humility on the one hand, and on the other his great erudition and outstanding learning coupled with a marvelous temperament and other gifts of character that could have brought him fame and honor in the eyes of men,[26] he could not help but marvel greatly and be deeply moved and filled with emotion that cannot be expressed either in writing or in speech. The Father used to make that kind of reflection in similar situations, and he drew much fruit from them, so that he clearly understood that he was profoundly unworthy of such holy companionship and social intercourse. Indeed, the more frequently he thought this way, the more he experienced in himself an increase in devotion and an increase in the need to show well-deserved reverence for servants of God like this.

[55] But, to return to the context of the narrative, that day the companions collected so much in alms that they not only drive away their

---

[25] Rodrigues. *FN* 3:74[21].

[26] It is not clear who this second companion is. Some think it is Laínez, some Xavier, and at least one author thinks it is a combination of both Laínez and Xavier!

hunger with a happy and frugal meal fitting to the poor, but at the same time they also have enough to redeem the pawned breviary.

[56] Finally they come to the blessed shrine of Our Lady of Loreto.[27] After spending two or three days in devotional meditations and prayers,[28] they head for Rome. They had a very difficult time on the journey, lots of rain, and muddy roads. It happened that three companions[29] consumed one whole day in fasting, walking without food, wet and muddy. Finally, on a dark and gloomy night when they could not beg for alms, they reach the fortified town of Tolentino. While the Fathers were entering the town, one of them,[30] going neither to right or left, went straight ahead where there was the most mud, saying to himself over and over, "If the rains come pouring down, I'll not get any wetter. Even though the streets are muddier, I can't get any muddier." While he was thinking this a little after entering the town, a man meets him right in the middle of the mire, tall, handsome, wearing a hat, his mouth covered by a long mantle wound around his neck. Without saying anything he took the Father by the hand, then he reaches out, puts some silver coins in his hand, and squeezes it shut, then leaves and goes on farther as though he was going some place. Father judged, not from his face, which he could not see, but from his height and strong frame, that he was thirty years old, and certainly not

[27] Schurhammer suggests the following chronology: 16 March leave Venice; 18 Ravenna; 19 morning departure; 20 morning arrival Ancona, departure toward noon, evening arrival Loreto; 21 departure except for Rodrigues and two companions; 21 Tolentino; 22 departure; 22 Foligno; 23 Terni; 24 Città Castellana; 25 Rome. This schedule requires 31 miles (50 km) per day except for the Tolentino-Foligno section, which is 37 miles (60 km). *FN* 3:74[23].

[28] The companions stayed in the hospice of St. Benignus, where there is a hospice today. *FN* 3:75[24]. There is a plaque at Loreto listing all the saints and blesseds who have visited there and, if the present translator is not mistaken, Faber's name leads all the rest, or is very near the top of the list. *GS* 320[59]: "The marble enclosure of the Holy House of Loreto, with its fine reliefs, which were begun in 1513, was almost finished . . . in 1537. The statues of the sybils and the prophets, which were begun in 1540, were not there. The beautiful drawing of the south side with the adoration of the shepherds and of the wise men by Francisco d'Olanda still shows the empty niches."

[29] Rodrigues and two others who accompanied him to Tolentino. The rest set out from Loreto the next day after their arrival, which is shown from Bobadilla's testimony that they arrived in Rome on Palm Sunday, 25 March, not enough time for that long a journey if they had stayed in Loreto two or three days. *FN* 3:75[24]. Rodrigues and his companions arrived in Rome in the middle of Holy Week.

[30] Rodrigues. FN 76[25].

much more, his carriage manly and upright. Thinking no more about it, Father kept his hand closed until he reached the hospice. When he got there he opened his hand and found what seemed enough for supper. As soon as the other two companions, who had gone down the side streets of the town, see the money they say, "We saw that man talking with you, but we thought he was asking who we were." While the Fathers are talking, a beggar who was in the same hospice says to them, "My good men, it is late already, and you are not familiar with this place. If you are to eat today, I am free, and while there is time and the taverns are open, I'll buy what is needed and bring you whatever you want." Taking the coins, he brought bread, wine, and dried figs, which sufficed for the Fathers' supper and to give some to the poor. And so they all ate and gave thanks to God who takes care of the poor even in the least things.

> *Commentary:* Is the donor of the money the same young man of 30 years of age who encountered the companions in [40] above? The man is not recognizable for Simão cannot see his face. Think also of the disciples on the way to Emmaus in Luke 24:13-35. On a day whose dark and stormy weather matches the disciples' interior disposition this man gives Simão something. After the man is gone, Simão recognizes an alms sufficient for him and his companions to break bread together, with a little left over for the poor (shades of the feeding of the multitude). At least Simão sees the providential action of God in both instances.

[57] When they reached Rome[31] each one went to the hospice for his

---

[31] *GS* 322[69]: "The road from Tolentino over the Apennines went then, as it does today, by way of Belforte, Valcimara, Valdica, Muccia, and Gelagna to Serravalle. It then turned left to go around the marshes by way of Taverne (the modern road goes to the right and climbs the steep country in sweeping curves) to Cifo, Casenove, Scopoli, and Pale. From there the dangerous old road followed the steep precipices (whereas the new one runs high above on the left) to Foligno." N. 70: "Here the road ran again into the Via Flaminia, which was usually followed by all travelers from here to Rome." If I follow *GS* 322-23, they went from Foligno to Trevi to Spoleto to Narni, looked down from dizzy heights above the white-foaming Nera, then past ancient Otricoli down to the Tiber, crossed by boat to get to Bhorghetto, then on to Città Castellana. On the last day of their journey Mt. Soracte was on their left. They passed through Rignano and Castelnuovo, reached the inn of Prima Porta, crossed the old Roman Ponte Molle.

own nationality.[32] But someone of those who visited the Roman curia said that our men had come to ask for favors, and others were saying that surely they were fugitives, deserters from religious orders, and had come to the City to get rid of their habit. But to those who asked them why they had come to Rome the Fathers replied: for reasons of devotion, to visit the Churches and to see the holy places of the city of Rome because they were outstanding. They conversed with everyone about divine things and fed themselves on what they gathered from door to door. And so some of the people in the curia, Spaniards and wealthy men,[33] formed a good opinion of our men, and they welcomed both the Spaniards and the French at the hospice of St. James, asserting that it would not be to their honor or to that of Spain if they permitted these men to beg alms from door to door, and so from then on they always supplied the Fathers what they needed for food, not much but sufficient, and they did not refuse for it made it easier for them to visit the sacred sights and religious places.

[58] In Rome at this time a certain doctor of theology from Paris, a Spaniard by the name of Pedro Ortiz, a learned and virtuous man, was engaged in some business with the Sovereign Pontiff. He had been sent to the City by Charles V.[34] Learning that the companions had come to Rome, he goes to the Sovereign Pontiff Paul III and informs him that nine theologians from Paris are in Rome (for Ignatius had remained in Venice)[35] who have inspired great hopes in him, men who really practice poverty and are determined to sail for Jerusalem. The

[32] The hospice for Spaniards was San Giacomo degli Spagnoli; for the French, San Luigi dei Francesi; for the Portuguese, San Antonio dei Portoghesi; there was no national church and hospice for the Savoyards, but since Francis I, the French king, had taken Savoy in 1536, Faber and Jay had a right to go to San Luigi dei Francesi. See what Rodrígues says a little below about the companions who were accepted at San Giacomo. *FN* 3:76[26].

[33] At the annual meeting, 28 December 1536, the following are named: Governor of the national hospice and its church, Juan Moedano, Auditor of the Rota; his consultors, Felipe de Agnelis, Abbreviatore della Presidenza Maggiore, Doctor of theology Pedro Ortiz, the imperial legate, and Juan Martínez de Anguiano and Martín de Aguinaga, Doctor of civil and canon law. The administrators were Luis de Torres and Antoniotto de la Salde. *FN* 3:78[27].

[34] Ortiz was sent to Rome by Charles V in 1531 to defend the rights of Catharine of Aragon, the wife of Henry VIII. When the queen died in 1536, Paul III kept Ortiz in Rome for ecclesiastical purposes, especially to prepare the council (Trent). Ortiz was at that time a consultor at the hospice for Spaniards, San Giacomo. *FN* 3:79[29].

[35] Ignatius stayed in Venice because he had expected that both Giovanni Pietro Carafa and Pedro Ortiz would be unfriendly in Rome. *FN* 3:79[30].

Pontiff responds, "Bring them to me tomorrow. See to it also that some other theologians are present for I will be delighted to hear these men disputing on theological questions during dinner." Ortiz carries out the commands. Next day the companions are on hand, and in the presence of the Sovereign Pontiff while he is dining, many theologians who were already sitting at his table press now this Father, now that one, on some theological matter.[36] As he had said beforehand, the Pontiff arose from table happy and content at the end of the disputation. When he gets up the companions immediately kneel at his feet, and when they have all kissed his feet, the Roman Pontiff with his arms wide open as though he wanted to embrace them all, spoke in Latin, "I experience great happiness and joy when I see erudition like this joined with great modesty. If you need anything within my power, I shall gladly grant it." They say, "We humbly request only your blessing and permission to go to Jerusalem." The Pontiff replied, "I gladly grant you this. Nevertheless I believe you are not likely to get to Jerusalem." The Pontiff said this either because he knew the Venetians were going to arm themselves against the Turks, which happened a little later, or because he was high priest that year [cf. Jn. 11:51]. In this manner he dismissed them.[37] The companions who were not yet ordained were kindly given permission to be ordained by any bishop on three consecutive feast days, and their "erudition" was allowed to substitute for "sufficient income" [as a title for ordination].[38] Besides, they received money twice from the Pontiff of his own accord without anyone's requesting it, and a sum of more than 210 ducats was gathered by other Spaniards against expenses for sailing to Joppa and for other taxes imposed by the Turks.[39] This money was transferred to Venice by merchants' letters at no cost. Later on, after they had lost all hope of sailing to Jerusalem, the money was returned to the Sovereign Pontiff and the other Spaniards through the help of Ortiz. The Pontiff marveled at this and did not accept the money, but the Fathers did not make use of it.

[36] According to a letter from Ignatius to Jean de Verdolay, 24 July 1537, present on that occasion and asking them questions were papal legates, cardinals, bishops, learned men [*EI* 1:119]. For an account of those who attended discussions and disputations at the pope's table, cf. *TV* II/1, 83-84. Remember that only Faber, Broët, Jay, and Hozes were priests. All of them must have been amazed and a bit startled to find themselves in that company.

[37] Their request was granted through Cardinal Pucci, Paenitentiario Maiore, 27 April. *FN* 3:80[34]. See [L39].

[38] Cardinal Pucci also signed dimissorial letters that same day so that they could be ordained. *FN* 3:80, n. 35.

[39] *FN* 3:80[36].

CHAPTER FIVE: Republic of Venice, 1537-38

[59] I had intended to bring this to an end at this point, for I am not unaware that what should be written down after this is better known and has been written by someone else.[1] Nevertheless I shall write down little bits from here and there that are not sufficiently known to everyone, or certainly not thoroughly spelled out, as they say.

[60] They returned to Venice[2] where they were welcomed at their hospitals to the great joy and happiness of everyone. A little later, after devoutly taking vows of poverty and chastity[3] at the feet of a bishop who was the apostolic legate to the Venetians,[4] Father Ignatius, Francis Xavier, Diego Laínez, Alfonso Salmerón, John Codure, Nicolás Bobadilla, and Simão Rodrigues were initiated into sacred orders and received the dignity of the priesthood on the feast of John the Baptist by the bishop of Arbe.[5] Later he frankly admitted to some people that he had never experienced so much joy and consolation in ordaining.[6]

[61] Meanwhile, while the companions prepare to sail, a definite rumor of war to come starts around, the constant report that the Venetians had united with Paul III, the Supreme Pontiff, and Emperor Charles V against the Turks. Since all hope of sailing that year had been dashed because of the outbreak of war, the Fathers therefore decided to wait a whole year in order to show that their vow was genuine and discharge their promise.[7] Meanwhile, to prepare better for their first Masses, they decide to take some time out and to withdraw in twos and threes to secluded places far from people and to spend time in meditation and prayer. They did this in the area under the jurisdiction of Venice. For when they consulted men who were

---

[1] The reference is to Pedro Ribadeneira, *Vita P. Ignatii*, first published in 1572. *FN* 3:82[1].

[2] *GS* 338[216] says the route is unknown, perhaps back the way they came, or by way of Florence, Bologna, and Padua. Some may have gone one way, some the other. By this time Arias and Landívar had left the companions.

[3] Ignatius, too, indicates that they also took vows of chastity. [A93].

[4] Girolamo Veralli, pontifical legate to Venice from 1536. *FN* 3:82[2].

[5] Vincenzo Negusanti. *FN* 3:82[3.]

[6] [L 41].

[7] See [14] above.

familiar with the territory they judged that Vicenza, Treviso, Bassano, Verona, and Monteselice were especially suitable for solitude and reflection on the things of God. By lot, therefore, Fathers Nicolás Bobadilla and Paschase Broët go to Verona, and Fathers Ignatius, Faber, and Laínez to Vicenza.[8] They betake themselves to a monastery outside the city, once devastated by the whirlwind of war: solitary, abandoned, the doors torn off, the windows taken away.[9] Taking along a quantity of chaff, they spread it on the ground for sleeping, and beg alms from door to door.

[62] Father Claude Jay and Simão Rodrigues go to Bassano and find a man living in a small hermitage along with two companions. He was a solitary advanced in years, renowned for holiness, and long practiced in that way of living.[10] The old man had earlier stated categorically that he would not accept anyone into his community because some whom he had admitted had not been trustworthy. Nonetheless, he received our men in a friendly manner and indicated to his companions that he was unable not to admit them. The good old man said, "I felt so open to them, so compassionate, so moved, so ready to accept them, that I thought it would be criminal to exclude them." Indeed, the departure of the Fathers was so hard on him that we saw his face blanch because of it. Although with respect to eating and sleeping the Fathers led an austere life there, nevertheless they did not set aside the habit that priests usually wear. In that place, for a bed they lay on bare boards along with an ass the old man had to haul wine that he begged at harvest time and to gather the ripe harvest of wheat, a custom which that solitary had observed for a long time. Father Francis Xavier and Alfonso Salmerón came to another small shrine, abandoned and alone, situated on Monteselice.[11] It fell to Jean Codure and a certain Hozes who had joined the companions in Venice to come to

---

[8] These five, plus Xavier and Salmerón, had an hour's journey across the lagoon to Lizzafusina, and then "a seven-hour walk along the ship-laden Grand Canal brought them through fruitful plains sown with villages, inns, and elegant villas of Venetian nobles to Padua. The following day they set out on their separate ways." *GS* 349-50. Xavier and Salmerón walked south for four hours to Monselice. *GS* 350.

[9] San Pietro in Vivarolo. *FN* 3:84[7].

[10] Fra Antonio. *GS* 361 and 361[199].

[11] *GS* 351[104]: "This statement refers to the only chapel still standing on the mountain today, that of St. George, which is already mentioned in 1099 (Cognolato 53-54)." "Still standing" is a bit ambiguous, for *GS* says in the same note that it was torn down in 1592 and replaced with the "modern" one.

Treviso. At that time Father Ignatius lay sick at Vicenza. Simão Rodrigues, however, in that little shrine at Bassano began to become so sick that he seemed at death's door and the doctors completely despaired for his life. When Ignatius heard of this, he gets up from his straw in spite of his fever and sets out on the 16½ mile[12] journey from Vicenza to Bassano along with Peter Faber. On the way he recovered from his fever and sensed in the Spirit of God that the Father would not die from the illness that afflicted him. He immediately said so to Faber. Then when he came to the sick man, he told him to be of good heart, indicating that he certainly was not going to die of his sickness. Moreover, when he saw the sick man still dressed and lying on the boards, he saw to it that the ancient solitary made the effort to acquire a bed on which the sick Father could rest after undressing.[13]

[63] In these solitary cells the Fathers first began to practice obedience voluntarily. This is the way they did it. Whether in twos or threes, one of them was in charge of the other companions for a week, taking turns one after another. They were so obedient and submissive to the one in command that they seemed more bound by vow than by sheer freedom. Later when they all were by now in Rome together, they decided to extend the command to a month, which lasted until the election of Father Ignatius as General. During all that time he diligently obeyed just like all the rest. The others nevertheless always judged it proper to treat him with special reverence.

[64] The time had not yet passed that the Fathers had set aside for solitude when all the Fathers came together to Ignatius at Vicenza so that they might determine with him how to spend the rest of the time before the time for sailing to Jerusalem would be upon them. They all gathered together in that ruined old monastery. There the Fathers slept in a room almost totally covered with straw. At night they would block up the windows with fragments of the ancient walls and by day remove them so that the light could come in (for the doors were

[12] *GS* 362 says the distance was 22 miles. In both Latin and Portuguese Rodrigues says 18 (Roman) miles.

[13] The hermitage was outside the walls of Bassano "on the street which led over the covered wooden bridge to Val Sugana" (*GS* 362). *GS* 362[200] says the hermitage is still there, and continues: "The chapel adjoining the church has three modern frescoes commemorating Fra. Antonio, Rodrigues, and St. Ignatius's visit. It was once the room in which the hermit lived, an old, half-fallen tower."

always open without any hinges). For food they begged from door to door, as was their custom, enough to sustain life. On occasion they would preach in the piazzas.

[65] Some of the companions offered their first Masses here; Father Ignatius said his first Mass later in Rome, and another Father likewise in Ferrara.[14] Two fell sick.[15] Admitted into a hospital for incurables, they were given one bed so narrow they could hardly fit in it, so they had plenty of opportunity to practice patience. It frequently happened that one of them would be burning with fever and want to throw off the covers while the other was suffering from chill and wanted to keep them. But each bore his suffering cheerfully and tried to make it easier for the other rather than for himself. These Fathers were lying in this huge hospital, poor and open to the winds, separated from the main hospital for incurables,[16] when one night St. Jerome appeared to one of them who thought he was awake.[17] He was greatly devoted to him, and he appeared grave, venerable, worthy of great reverence, consoling him with these friendly words, "You will pass the winter in Bologna and will be tossed about by many storms of suffering," which is what happened.[18] For there he fell into a very strong quartan fever, and from the cold, the poverty, and the lack of everything, he became so thin and pale, so changed from what he had been, that he did not seem to be alive but was like a cadaver. When I saw him later in Rome, so thin, feeble, almost worn out, I did not think that it was possible for him to recover his original health and vigor. I was completely convinced that he would never be able to work again. "As for the other

[14] At San Pietro in Vivarolo: Xavier, Laínez, Bobadilla, Codure; Rodrigues celebrated his first Mass in Ferrara; Salmerón had not yet been ordained; Ignatius delayed his first Mass until Christmas Eve of 1538. Salmerón was not ordained until the end of October or beginning of November. *FN* 3:88[13].

[15] Xavier and Rodrigues. *FN* 3:89[14]. *GS* 368.

[16] This was the hospital called Santa Maria della Misericordia, in the charge of the so-called Compagnia secreta di San Girolamo (St. Jerome). From the time that under the direction of St. Cajetan Thiene it accepted those afflicted with syphilis, it began to be called also the hospital of the incurables. Connected to it was another house that had three beds for poor pilgrims. *FN* 3:89[15].

[17] Francis Xavier. *FN* 3:89[16]. *GS* 368.

[18] *GS* 368[238]: "The apparition is the subject of a picture which the director of the hospital, Guerra, had painted in 1738 (picture in Poli, *La prima Messa* 372). Today it is in the *Ospidale Civico San Bortolo* in Vicenza. . . . On the painting, whose inscription erroneously assumes that the apparition took place in the hospital of Sant'Antonio, see Poli, 'Intorno ad un'antica pittura raffigurante San Francesco Saverio,' *L'Avvenire d'Italia*, Dec. 4, 1930, p. 4."

companions," continued Jerome, "some will go to Rome, others to Padua, some to Ferrara, and others to Siena." While these two Fathers were absent suffering in the hospital, the other companions, not knowing what had happened to them, decided[19] that Father Ignatius, Faber and Laínez would go to Rome; Father Salmerón and Paschase Broët to Siena; to Bologna Francis Xavier, who suffered quartan fever there, and Nicolas Bobadilla; Father Claude Jay and Simão Rodrigues would go to Ferrara; and to Padua John Codure and Hozes, mentioned earlier.[20]

[66] Besides, before leaving for these cities, some of the Fathers returned to their solitary cells so that they might spend the whole intervening time in solitude in those deserted places. Finally, when the time was over, they set out for their towns in the way indicated above. And indeed almost all, establishing their domiciles in hospitals or places considered more appropriately suitable, passed the days in profound poverty, begging each day from door to door (not even enough bread was given to live on). In the churches and in the streets they urged people to detest sin, to keep the commandments of God and of the Church, exhorting them to frequent reception of the sacraments of confession and the Eucharist, which had almost fallen into disuse, as if buried in eternal oblivion. By the restoration and renewal of these sacraments very many improved their lives, and renouncing their former evil practices, they gave great thanks to God both for finding the hidden treasure and for the excellent and salutary medicine they had found for the salvation of their souls. At that time this was something new and unusual, and a source of amazement and edification to everyone, especially when the Fathers were seen as very

---

[19] These deliberations took place at San Pietro in Vivarolo in Vicenza during the month of October 1537. During these deliberations Ignatius first proposed the name of the group. St. Bernardine of Siena had given missions in Vicenza, had promoted devotion to the Holy Name of Jesus, and founded a confraternity to help the poor, the Compagnia del buon Gesù, still extant at the time of Ignatius. Another confraternity there had affiliated with itself a group of young candidates bearing the name, Compagnia dei Soldatelli di Gesù. Since the companions had no other head or leader than Jesus Christ, Ignatius suggested they identify themselves as the Compagnia di Gesù, the Society of Jesus. See *GS* 370-71.

[20] *GS* 370: "Inigo had astutely arranged the groups, combining the various nationalities, always putting a Frenchman with a Spaniard or Portuguese and an older priest with a younger one. For Bologna he had made an exception. The rough, brash, and impetuous Bobadilla needed a counterweight in the son of the former president of the Royal Council of Navarre."

eager to procure the salvation of everyone, sparing no vigils, no labors, not even themselves. But when the companions considered the rich harvest that the merciful Lord of the vineyard[21] was gathering, they counted the hunger and the cold and the rest of their labors as the sweetest delights of the soul and as singular signs of divine benefi- cence. To God therefore may thanks and praise be given for these many wonderful gifts.

[67] The companions spent the whole winter in the above-mentioned cities engaged in these occupations, and also the rest of the time before the year was completed for fulfilling their vow. I think that many things worthy of mention happened to them in these places, in fact I am practically sure of it. I could not know everything because we were in different places, and some of what I knew has escaped my memory in the course of time so that I dare not write them down. However, I shall conclude with a few little stories that have a stronger hold on my memory.

[68] At Padua where Codure and Hozes happened to go they fulfilled their sacred duties very carefully with great benefit to the citizens.[22] Divine providence wished to reward Hozes fittingly, worn out as he was by his labors. This is what happened. After Hozes had already preached many sermons to the people of Padua, he one day goes to the forum itself to preach, ablaze with a more fiery spirit, and on this text, "Watch and pray for you know not the hour when your Lord will come" [Mt 24:42]. He speaks passionately in an exciting and stirring oration. But almost immediately or very shortly after he falls sick and in the hospice for the poor he met the day of his death. At that moment, so I have heard from some of our men, Father Ignatius, who at the time was engaged in some business or other on Monte Cassino,[23] saw his soul going into heaven bathed in splendor and surrounded by brilliant light. Likewise, while he was saying Mass, when he came to the words in the Confiteor, "and all the saints," he saw clearly a great assembly of the blessed shining with brilliance on all sides, and

[21] Cf. the language Faber uses in his letter of 23 November 1538 to Gouveia, where he refers to the pope as "the lord of the universal harvest of Christ" [*EI* 132].

[22] The suffragan bishop threw them in jail in chains the first night, much to the delight of Hozes, but treated them as sons after he was better informed [L 43].

[23] Ignatius had come to Monte Cassino to direct Dr. Pedro Ortiz in the Spiritual Exercises. *FN* 3:93[22].

among them Hozes in supreme happiness. Hozes was born in Malaga, on fire with love and plainly indefatigable in the service of God and the salvation of his neighbor. Although he always showed forth shining proof of his goodness, he was even more ardently engaged in the works of the spirit when he died.

> *Commentary:* The word that is here translated "goodness" is "probitas." Does it refer to virtue in general or to participation in that Goodness of God which rules the Society: the Goodness that created out of chaos, that promised countless offspring to an old man named Abraham, that called the Israelites out of Egypt, that surprised the world with the Incarnation? The Middle Ages referred to chivalrous exploits as "probitates."[24] This sense of goodness springing from chivalrous dedication to and union with God seems to be the sense in which Simão uses the word, a sense easily applicable to each of the companions on his pilgrimage.

[69] Codure remained alone in Padua, profoundly moved by grief at the loss of his companion, and deeply distressed by the weight of many serious matters. What kind of love, then, was it which existed among the companions? How on fire was their love? To console Codure and to help him carry his burden, one of the two companions who were at Ferrara, a neighboring town, came to him immediately.[25] It was wonderful how much the coming of this Father soothed the heart of Codure, what powerful encouragement it gave him, what power it added to reap the bountiful harvest which the hard work of Hozes, in great part, had caused to grow while he was alive, and was brought to happy fruition through his loving memory now that he was dead. This Father who came to Codure did not return to Ferrara but stayed at Padua and went with Codure to Ignatius in Rome. Tied up in some works for the salvation of the citizens, they would come to Rome a little later than the others, as we shall say in the proper place.[27]

[70] And so that Father meantime was a help to Codure, and he also zealously went to work so that the hearts of the citizens of Padua would be formed in true zeal for God and zeal for his people. So it happened that all became bound to one another through mutual care

---

[24] See J. F. Niermeyer, *Mediae Latinitatis Lexicon Minus* (Leiden: Brill, 1984), 854a.

[25] Simão Rodrigues, who went to Padua in March or April. *FN* 3:94[23].

[26] See [79].

for each other, and found theselves enhanced and enriched thereby.
For, to pass over the rest, one of the companions became very ill and
was received into the home of an ecclesiastic, a very wealthy nobleman, and was treated with generous hospitality.[27] That pious man had
profited so much from the Father's conversation and sermons that he
will often swear later that a year had passed since he ceased a relationship with a lady friend who lived with him inside the house, and by
whom he had borne a child. Not satisfied with this, the companions
persuade him to dismiss her from his home and locate her elsewhere
in a decent manner, and so it was.

[71] However, while the one was sick, the other zealously watched out
both for the health of his suffering companion and for the welfare of
his neighbors. He used to visit other homes and he was modestly provided for by a generous and pious widow and was courteously
heaped with many kindnesses. For the son of this widow, a very dig-
nified man with a prestigious doctorate, had often pleaded with her
that when he left to join some religious order she might take the Father
in his place. Another very dear son of this same widow who died not
so long ago, while he was dying recommended to his mother that this
very amiable Father to whom he was much indebted would sufficiently meet her need for a son.

[72] Yet the Fathers took little advantage of this kind of largesse, and
they did not want to accept any more than they judged necessary each
day for the simplest meal for poor men. Wherefore, when this noble
matron who had already gifted them abundantly offered on their
departure a lot of money and help for the journey, they insist that they
will take nothing for the trip. This good lady pleads and begs insis-
tently that they at least be willing to take some little handkerchiefs.
The Fathers agree lest they seem to despise her charitable desires. She,
therefore, prepares some little handkerchiefs but quietly and secretly
enfolds money, cleverly concealing it in the folds of the handkerchiefs.
So she brings these seemingly simple little gifts to the companions,
and they, totally unaware of this well-intentioned subterfuge, accept
the gift with thanks and, saying goodbye to the woman, finally take
their leave. Later when they unfolded the handkerchiefs in the hospice
for the poor in Venice the deception was discovered, for all of a sudden the money falls out at their feet and begins to roll away. The

---

[27] Codure. *FN* 3:94[25].

companions found out from experience that the deceit took place through divine providence, for it later provided for them when in great need.

[73] When they had left Padua, therefore, not a little good will on the part of many followed them, to the extent that an important man, a canon of that city, could not be deterred from accompanying the Fathers. He did not simply go with them for a short distance beyond the city but he was in their company all the way to Venice and thence to Ancona and finally to Loreto (whether he also had a servant, I do not dare to say). He frequently marveled that the companions spent whole nights lying on the ground and led a very difficult life, and he complained that he often was dead weight for them because of his own softness and that their harshness of life was truly the happiness that he desired. This is what occurs to me about Padua.

[74] In a different city[28] another pair of companions at first suffered difficulties that were by no means insignificant, and left impressive evidence of their passionate zeal. For to come to the sufferings endured, they incontestably put up with the extreme violence of freezing cold, and bore in misery the fury of a severely threatening sky. For it was winter time and the days were stormy, the air frosty and exceedingly cold, the rains unceasing, the sky mostly cloudy when our men were in this city. Moreover, the hospice where they were taken in was not one of the better places but the poorest in the city. It was made of earth, a huge place, far too damp, and pervious to the blowing winds. This hospice was in the care of a sharp little old woman who would not allow anyone to go to bed clothed. As a matter of fact, before she would go to bed she made each of the poor people shed their clothes in her presence, even undergarments, to see if any were covered with sores or with any deadly blemishes they might pass on to others. The healthy ones there put their clothes on a bench far removed lest the sheets and blankets be contaminated by lice, and then went to bed. Even our men to whom only one bed was allotted in the hospice of the poor had to take off their clothes and go to sleep nude in the woman's presence. However, as best they could in these difficult circumstances, they covered their private parts decently. In the hospice, as soon as they were aroused from sleep, they got up,

---

[28] Ferrara, where Claude Jay and Simon Rodrígues had been sent. *FN* 3:96[26].

struck a spark from flint, lit a lamp, and dressed in their poor garments began to recite their morning prayers, and each night they
spent time in other prayers as well. The little old lady, however, carefully observed what the companions did quietly and in secret.
Noticing also that the Fathers ate very little and frequently instructed
the poor in the Christian faith, she persuaded herself that the men
were filled with the greatest sanctity, and later she often proclaimed
this publicly in the most exalted terms. For the Marchioness of
Pescara,[29] well-known and a very devout person, who happened to be
in the city at the time and was also preparing to go to Jerusalem to visit
the holy places, wanted to find out about the Fathers' religious commitment and integrity not in some haphazard way but clearly and
directly. And since she had often caught sight of these two in one of
the city's churches, she approached one of them one day and asked the
man if he was a member of that group of Paris theologians who were
waiting for an opportunity to sail to Jerusalem. When she found that
out she further asked where they were staying and learned it was the
hospice for the poor she goes at once while we were out and carefully
asks the woman taking care of the place who are these companions
and what are they like. And she responds in great detail: "Obviously
they are saints, and to be commended for their incorrupt morals, their
spotless lives, and the purity of their doctrine. They do not eat, nor do
they drink, they spend the whole night in prayer and meditation. I
have seen them, I myself have seen them often while I was spying on
them very carefully." Therefore, after that they accepted food from the
Marchioness and through her intervention they were transferred to
another more commodious hospice for the poor where they had a
room and a bed, bread each night, not much, but they began to eat a
little better. For no matter how much hunger and lack of almost everything they suffered at first, it had certainly long been embraced in
prayer. And so I move forward a bit.

> *Commentary:* Both the vocabulary and the content of the first
> sentence are strikingly similar to what is found in the last sen-
> tence of [68] above. Both speak of evidence (*specimen/vestigia*) of
> virtue (*probitas*), and both speak of passion (*ardentius/ardoris*).
> These are the qualities to be found in the valiant knight of the
> Middle Ages who performed mighty deeds.

[29] Vittoria Colonna. *FN* 3:97[27]. The devout Lydia in Acts 16:14-15 comes to mind.

[75] They kept working hard to rid the city of vice and they put all their thought and energy into creating enthusiasm for matters of the spirit. And so they frequently preached, had salutary conversations with many in private, often brought the Eucharist, and allowed no opportunity to escape them for doing something good.

[76] Wherefore, the suffragan bishop of the city,[30] from whom our men had received no kindness or favor, finally became aware of the integrity of their lives and that there was no reason to be suspicious of them. He approaches them in a very loving manner and kindly offers them himself and all his resources. He protests at length how stirred he is by benevolent love for them, and on occasion invites them to his table in the following weeks.

[77] One day when they were all seated at table, this great prelate addresses the Fathers with great charm in this manner: "You will pardon me," he says, "that although I am the person who is responsible for providing patronage for any good works, I have never given anything to assist you in your labors, nor have I ever promoted your most laudable efforts by any sign of favor. No wonder, however, if you catch my meaning, since everything human is being tossed about on the waves of error, so much fraud is masked and hidden maliciously that nothing appears so sacred and holy that a wise and reasonable person could not be suspicious of it. I myself knew a preacher not so long ago, outstanding from a religious point of view, a powerful and effective preacher, well known for his sanctity. So he preaches to the people. Many people come, celebrities, people in positions of authority, those known for their prudence and wisdom or for their learning or for the integrity of their lives. He impels their hearts wherever he wishes and especially he moves them to lamentations and tears. But what was he really like, this man otherwise adorned with all praise? At this very time when he was touted in the eyes and on the lips of all, he had a young girl dressed in men's clothing, his partner in the most awful sins of impurity who always went with him as his companion. Furthermore, it sometimes happened that while he was in the pulpit giving an impassioned sermon everyone in the church would be wailing in a phenomenal way. On returning home he says to the girl, "What do you think? Didn't I provoke abundant tears in the

---

[30] Ottaviano del Castello, vicar of Cardinal Giovanni Salviati. *FN* 3:103⁴.

listeners?" And she says, "You provoked the tears of those who know you only on the outside. Arouse them in me who already know you intimately." The preacher, therefore, made a solemn promise obliging himself to make her wail at the next sermon. She smiled, but on the designated day the preacher addressed the people with such vim and vigor that in the midst of all the weeping together, he compelled the woman (even though she fought against it) to great weeping and wailing." Thus far the bishop, more or less. "So you can see," he says, "most loving Fathers, whether one can easily trust in the appearance of religious fervor or in what looks like virtue." But let us pass over all this and similar happenings to the Fathers in various towns.

CHAPTER SIX: Rome, 1538-39

[78] The year passed which they were bound by vow to wait to sail to Jerusalem; the war between the Christians and the Turks grew stronger day by day; the Fathers come together to Ignatius who was living in Rome so that they might all together give an account of themselves and their affairs to the Supreme Pontiff as they had determined, and to treat with one another concerning other matters relating to their future plans and the reasons supporting them. Meanwhile Father Ignatius along with his companions Faber and Laínez had found a place to stay in the home and vineyard of Quirino Garzoni, a man of great virtue.[1] When some of our friends found out that the other companions were coming to Rome they rented for some months another larger house in a better location, persuading Ignatius that if they left the old one which was located somewhat off the beaten track (for it was situated not far from the monastery of the Most Holy Trinity), they could move there in a location near the center of the city which seemed more suitable for the Society's ministries.[2]

[79] The new house is accepted, and they all finally congregate there after Easter. For although many had already come from their towns before Easter, those in Padua arrived later.[3] Hence they began to preach even before informing the Sovereign Pontiff of their plans,[4] sometimes in churches, sometimes in the public streets, urging the people to do penance for their sins, to embrace our most gracious God with the fullest love, and to frequent the sacraments of Confession and

---

[1] The house now belongs to the Resurrectionists, Via Sebastianello, n. 11. *GS* 408[11].

[2] We get some idea of the location of this house only from what Nadal says of it: "After experiencing the limitations of this first house, they moved to another near the Ponte Sisto and the house of Dr. Ortiz." *FN* 2:169[3]. "Near the Ponte Sisto" is as close as we can come to locating it.

[3] Codure and Rodrigues. Rodrigues was sent to Padua after Hozes died. *FN* 3:103[4].

[4] In the preceding paragraph Rodrigues had said that they intended to give an account of themselves and their plans when they came to Rome. As indicated above, they did not all gather in Rome until after Easter, April 21. The pope left Rome for Nice on March 23. *GS* 419. The faculties were granted on May 3 by the papal legate, Vincent Carafa. *FD* 537-39. They started preaching on May 5. *GS* 425.

the Eucharist.[5] The Roman populace was so moved to do this that all the Fathers could hardly satisfy the crowds that came. The fervor and zeal of the companions was such that they were unmindful of food and so forgetful of themselves that unless they returned from the churches at dinner time they did not remember that they ought to take something to sustain themselves. But when they did not find anything to eat, they would leave the house to gather what they could from street to street, already well worn out and at a time of day most inopportune for begging alms. They did all this work with the greatest joy in their hearts. At the same time two Fathers were teaching theology at the Sapienza in Rome.[6] One was explaining the various senses of Scripture, and the other discussed what they call "theological questions" to the delight of everyone. Frequently called by the Sovereign Pontiff, they gathered with other doctors of the Sapienza to discuss various difficult theological issues at table, at which time the Pontiff showed special regard for us. At that time it was so unheard of and so unusual for clerics to ascend the pulpit that many people, overcome with astonishment, would say, "We always thought that monks were the only ones who could preach." Besides the usual works in which the companions were involved, many other special ones offered themselves, so that they became usual and ordinary. They became so many in number, that they cannot be described. Therefore I shall pass over these works, especially since someone else has written about them.[7]

[80] One, however, I shall insert into this letter. One winter in Rome [1538] the food supply was so unstable, the cold so harsh and unbearable, that the poor in the rows of houses and in the city squares were freezing and were breathing their last at night from starvation, deprived of all human help. No one took care of them, no one received them into hospices, no one was to be found who was moved

---

[5] "Ignatius preached in Spanish in Santa Maria de Monserrate, the others in Italian more or less: Faber in San Lorenze in Damaso, Jay with great satisfaction in the [French] church of Saint Louis, Salmerón in Santa Lucia [not clear which of many], Simão in San Angelo in Pescheria, Bobadilla in a church 'en Bancos' [San Celso], Laínez in San Salvatore in Lauro [L47]." See also *FN* 1:125[32].

[6] Faber and Laínez, the former teaching Scripture and the latter scholastic theology. *FN* 3:103[5]. Localed on the Corso del Rinascimento, n. 40, the university boasts a beautiful courtyard.

[7] Pedro Ribadeneira,*Vita P. Ignatii*, 1572. *FN* 3:105[6]. See above, Chapter Five, note 1.

by their wretched plight. Therefore, moved by compassion for them, the Fathers came to their help in their terrible need insofar as they could. At night they searched out those lying afflicted in the public squares, brought them home, washed their feet, begged from the devout as much bread as they needed to sustain life. They searched diligently for wood to build a fire for them and hay to couch them on the ground. Finally, they carefully instructed the ignorant in Christian doctrine and at times taught them prayers they should have known but of which they were totally ignorant. In the morning the poor went out to beg alms, and their number at one time grew to three or four hundred and the house could scarcely hold them. This action caused great admiration among the people and aroused some well known men who had a superabundance of everything, and even some cardinals, to imitate their zeal. For they said, "Aren't we ashamed that poor men, who do not even have food to eat, have done this wonderful, outstanding, holy thing? And we who have everything are doing nothing of the kind?" Because of this they collected a lot of money, and through the Fathers' diligence the needy were taken to a larger place where they were treated better than usual. In their zeal our men met not only the needs of those lying in the rows of houses and the byways but also the needs of about two thousand in various buildings who were reduced to terrible straits. Why, even the rulers of the city bought grain and worked with the citizens so that they would not be overwhelmed by high prices, and freed from this danger they lived peacefully with an abundance of grain and other things.

[81] Before the events that I have narrated took place the companions moved from that rented place—for the time of the contract[8] had run out—into another in which no one wanted to live, for it had a bad reputation among the people for ghosts and nocturnal specters.[9] This house was made available to the Fathers to live in in such a manner that they had no way of knowing who donated it or whether it was possessed by an evil spirit.[10] Nevertheless, when they were already about to move in and some benches, tables, and chairs had been sent ahead, one Father was assigned as custodian. He closed the doors and

[8] See [78].

[9] This was the house known as Frangipani. *FN* 3:107[9].

[10] It belonged to Antonino (or Antonio) Frangipani, a nobleman. He died in 1546 and his sepulcher is in the Church of St. Marcello. *FN* 3:107[10]. It is now called Palazzo Delfini, and is on Via dei Delfini, n. 16. *GS* 433[207].

while he was sleeping, suddenly heard an awful racket and horrible screaming, and said to himself, "If these are thieves, they have little or nothing to steal; if they are demons, they will do me no violence except what God permits; why, if God perhaps wishes that they take my life, God's will be done." Having said this, despising the raging demon with its ridiculous jeering, he quietly went back to sleep. Finally, when all the companions were living in the house, they often thought at night that pots, platters, vases, and earthenware dishes were being smashed to bits, but nonetheless, when day came, they were found whole and entire. Now and then during the day and at night as well that vile spirit knocked on the doors of the rooms, but when they were opened no one was there.

[82] In this building one of the companions became seriously sick and every night he heard that shady ghost walking in the hall outside his room and he observed noticeable characteristics in the way it walked. Sometimes also the devil lifted a mat hanging at the doorway, and, sticking in his head, seemed to look around at what was going on inside. But the sick man, although he saw nothing, experienced it as though he could see it. I could recount here many other frightening things by which those noxious shades of hell tried in vain to induce fear in the hearts of the Fathers. But since that would require a lengthy exposition, I have decided to leave them buried in silence. Yet I cannot not but be amazed at two things, the first, that the Fathers often scoffed at the games and dirges of the devil, treating them as worthless trifles, and the second, that it did not even enter their minds to compel the shades through sacred rites to leave the building and stir up no more trouble. For them that terrifying ghost was a joke and an object of contempt. In this building it happened that one of the Fathers[11] was aroused from sleep one night and cried out holy and pious words in a loud voice and at the same time had a violent nosebleed. When the others asked about it, he remained silent. The companions, however, were of the opinion that the devil had taken him by the throat and tried to suffocate him. But after some days when one of the Fathers asked him about it, he replied that he had dreamt that he had been drawn into an impure act and, after he was finally awakened by the tremendous effort he had made to resist, his nose had started to bleed profusely.

[11] Francis Xavier. *FN* 3:109[11].

[83] During this period some priests endowed with great virtue and on fire with a burning zeal wanted to join our men. The companions thought the matter should be referred first to the Supreme Pontiff. They meet with him and indicate that they can hardly extricate themselves from frequently hearing confessions and from many other activities. They ask him, therefore, for faculties to admit those who desired to join them. The Pontiff replies that it seems good to him, and therefore he kindly imparts to all his blessing and says that he cannot help but be greatly delighted at this turn of events. The Father took care that no document needed to be prepared. Because they had not yet explained to the Sovereign Pontiff what they were trying to set in motion, they wanted first of all, before they informed him of their intentions, to ponder much more thoroughly over some things that needed to be decided and which were later put into the document of the first confirmation of the Society, as will be told later.

[84] At this time in Rome a storm arose against our men, so serious and violent that many were convinced, indeed did not hesitate to assert, that our men should be burned at the stake, others that they should be sent into distant exile, and others that they should be condemned to suffer in the galleys. By means of these threats and terrors the evil enemy of the human race compelled two priests, who a little earlier had joined the companions, to flee full speed from the City.[12] I do not doubt that this common enemy of humanity had tried to drive the companions from the City by means of those ghosts and goblins. But they, undeterred, were unconcerned about the fugitive priests, laughed at the empty public rumors and said, "If it is established that we are heretics let us pay the penalty with fire, but if we are judged innocent, the judgment itself will testify that it is clear to all that our reputation has been disparaged beyond what is just and right, and that these charges have been falsely imputed against us." Indeed, they even indicated to Paul III, the Roman Pontiff, that they strongly desired and humbly begged that they all be bound in chains and cast into prison in the meanwhile until the truth of the alleged charges

---

[12] One of these was Lorenzo García, whose name is mentioned among the other companions in the document signed by Vincenzo Cardinal Carafa on 3 May 1538 granting the companions faculties. FD 538-39. From his letter to Ignatius of 1 February 1539 it appears that he was living with the companions in the house of Quirino Garzoni. EM 1:15-16. On 11 May 1538 he testified on behalf of Ignatius and his companions. EM 1:16-17. FN 3:110[13].

came to light, so that no one would be able to suspect that they would flee or set a foot outside the City. "It is not right," they said, "that by our sluggishness and lack of concern the works we are discerning to undertake for the Church should be reduced to nought and that what the ardent fire of zeal had accomplished, false accusations brought by certain men might dissipate." To this the Supreme Pontiff replied, "There has already been a thorough investigation of your way of living and the calumny of your detractors is pellucidly clear to me." For the Pontiff, who did everything with the greatest wisdom and prudence, had already seen to it secretly that the life and manner of living of the companions should be examined. But while the Fathers were being tossed about by the winds and the waves, they decided to remain in Rome so that no one would think they were planning to flee, and also to explain to the Sovereign Pontiff the thoughts that were in their minds, and again that they might look at their lives more reflectively. During that whole time no one went elsewhere to preach or to work in the Lord's vineyard, but all without exception stayed together in Rome.

[85] So that we grasp the origins of this calumny from its very beginning, this is what it was all about. During those days there was preaching at Rome a Piedmontese by the name of Agostino,[13] an Augustinian friar, an eloquent man, who was secretly giving the people of Rome to drink the poison of those heresies in which many are indulging today. Two Spanish priests were very devoted to him.[14] They were men of high standing, of great wealth, well known in the Roman curia, and they also seemed to embrace our men with special love. And so it came about that the companions did not hesitate to warn them not to put much faith in this monk's teaching and counsel. They who perhaps at that time had already been imbibing this poison received the warning so poorly that from friends they were immediately made adversaries. They began to disparage our reputation scurrilously, to oppose us enviously, and finally to inveigh against us abusively. Hence when all these unproved rumors were spread abroad, it was asserted repeatedly everywhere that the Fathers had fled as condemned heretics from Spain and Paris and Venice.

---

[13] Agostino Mainardi. *FN* 3:112[14].
[14] Pedro de Castilla and Francisco Mudarra. *FN* 3:112[14].

[86] There lived at that time in the City a student from Paris, a native of Navarre, who had been a servant of Father Francis Xavier in Paris. He was of average ability in the arts, and had, as they say, gotten a little taste of theology, but was somewhat inconstant in being faithful to a good decision.[15] When this man learned that the companions had set out for Rome, he followed and met them in Venice. There he obstinately begs them to accept him into their companionship and into their number. The Fathers, aware of his lack of talent, deny that it was in any way possible. The student then without any hope of the companionship of the Fathers makes friends in Rome with the Spanish priests. Along with them, almost insane in his attitude toward our men, he draws up an immense number of charges, and he is not afraid to assert that they are unworthy men. And so, to conclude briefly, after several days the lies were found out, the Navarrese was condemned on the charge of calumny by the Governor of the City, and because of wickedly daring to brand the Fathers with infamy he is finally banished from the City. Both Spaniards, on the other hand, are convicted of heresy. One of them, who broke out of prison to escape being burned at the stake, was burned in effigy in Rome.[16] The other was kept in jail for life. Coming to his senses toward the end of his life, and recognizing that he had strayed from the true faith, he renounced his former deeds in bitter sorrow and finally died after being helped by one of our Fathers in the final moments of his life.[17] It was discovered that he admitted being a teacher and strong defender of the most pernicious Lutheran teaching.[18]

[87] Meantime, while the rumor is getting about that the Fathers had fled from Spain, Paris, and Venice because of heresy and that for the same reason they are said to have been burnt in effigy in Spain, there came to Rome at one and the same time (an extraordinary thing that we believe happened through the providence of God) the Inquisitor of

---

[15] Miguel Landívar. *FN* 3:113[15].

[16] Francisco Mudarra. See *FN* 3:112[14] for the name. *FN* 3:112 erroneously has two n. 17's in the text but omits the first n. 17 in the notes. It should have contained some note on Mudarra.

[17] Pedro de Castilla. Diego de Avellaneda helped him die in prison in 1559. *FN* 3:113[17].

[18] Rodrigues is incorrect. Agostino Mainardi fled to the Valtellina valley in northern Italy and established a church in Chiavenna. He died an octogenarian on 31 July 1563. *FN* 3:113[18].

the Faith in Paris, Mathieu Ory, a Dominican who had thoroughly investigated the lives of the Fathers in Paris,[19] Juan Figueroa, the vicar general at Alcala for the Archbishop of Toledo, who had shown himself a diligent and trustworthy judge in investigating the life and teaching of Ignatius, and likewise Gasparo de Dotti, the vicar general of Venice, who had passed judgment in favor of Ignatius in the same city when some worthless but false charges had been maliciously brought against him. Each of them, called to testify strictly according to law before the Roman Governor (who carefully inquired about the teaching, manner of living, and the life of the Fathers), said many things in praise of them and fully commended their virtue and holiness. Not only those who had come from Spain, but from France and Venice as well, explained the care they had taken in investigating their way of living, extolling with much praise their virtue and example, and testified that in all things they had found them always to be genuine sons of the Catholic Church. And so, after interrogating these three witnesses who were beyond criticism, and many other witnesses as well, the Roman Governor clearly pointed out that this calumny was totally without foundation and had been thought up by a common enemy of the infant Society for the purpose of destroying it or certainly discrediting it, and pronounced the following judgment:[20]

JUDGMENT

[88] Benedetto Conversini, Bishop of Bertinoro, Vicar General of the beloved City and the Governor of the general district.

To all and to each to whom these letters shall come, health in the Lord.

Since it is very important for a Christian state that those be publicly recognized who bring many to salvation by their life, teaching, and example in the vineyard of the Lord, and likewise those who on the contrary rather try to sow weeds; and since some rumors have been spread abroad and delations made to us concerning the teach-

---

[19] Matthew Ory investigated Ignatius in Paris in 1529. *FN* 3:115[19].

[20] Ignatius asked for many copies of this judgment to send to his friends and benefactors. *FN* 3:115[20].

ing, and way of living, and the spiritual exercises which they conduct for others of the venerable men, Don Ignatius of Loyola and his companions, namely, Peter Faber, Claude Jay, Paschase Broët, Diego Laínez, Francis Xavier, Alfonso Salmerón, Simão Rodrigues, John Codure, and Nicolás Bobadilla, masters of Paris, secular priests of the dioceses of Pamplona, Geneva, Sigüenza, Toledo, Viseu, Embrun, and Palencia; whose teaching and exercises were said by some to be erroneous, superstitious, and on some points abhorrent to Christian doctrine: We, by reason of our office, and also by a special mandate of our Most Holy Lord, the pope, diligently taking note of these charges, have inquired into those matters that seemed relevant to shed further light on the case, should we find truth in the accusations.

Wherefore, after examining first of all some of those who placed charges against them, and after taking into consideration both public testimony and official judgments made in Spain, Paris, Venice, Vicenza, Bologna, Ferrara, and Siena in favor of the aforesaid Don Ignatius and his venerable companions and against their accusers, and in regard to these matters having examined judicially several witnesses who in character, teaching, and dignity were beyond all criticism, we find that the murmuring and accusations and rumors spread against them have no foundation in truth.

Therefore, we have judged that it is for us to pronounce and declare, as we do now pronounce and declare, that the aforesaid Don Ignatius and his companions have not only not incurred any stain of infamy either in law or in fact by reason of these accusations and rumors, but rather have achieved an even greater splendor in their lives and teaching, since we have certainly seen their adversaries make charges that were empty and far from the truth, and very solid men, on the contrary, bear excellent testimony on their behalf.

We think, therefore, that this judgment and pronouncement should be made so that it may be a public testimony on their behalf against all adversaries of the truth, and may also serve as a source of tranquillity for all who might have conceived that unfavorable suspicion against them on the basis of these vilifiers and accusers. Moreover, we advise, exhort in the Lord, and request that each and every one of the faithful should have and hold the abovementioned Don Ignatius and his venerable companions to be such as we have found them to be, and Catholics, and let every suspicion come to an end, in such a way that with God's help, which we hope for, they may persevere in the same manner of life and doctrine.

Given in our offices in Rome, November 18, 1538.

Signed: Benedetto, Governor
Signed: Rutilius Futius, Secretary.

Commentary: In his *Autobiography* Ignatius says that the papal legate wanted to impose silence on this whole affair, but Ignatius objected and wanted an official judgment rendered. Although even his friends objected that there was no need, Ignatius insisted, and when the pope returned to the city Ignatius requested a trial and the pope granted his request. Ignatius wanted no suspicion of heresy hanging over the companions. St. Paul objected that the police had thrown Roman citizens in jail without a trial and now wanted to dismiss them secretly (Acts 16:35-39). He also appealed to the emperor when Jewish enemies falsely accused him before Festus (Acts 25:1-12).

[89] So when the waves had calmed down and the storm that had arisen against the Fathers had dispelled itself, the dark cloud which had spread over the hearts of men disappeared. They began to see light and to set aside totally the adverse opinion they had conceived of our men now that the false whispers and rumors that had been going about the City were dispersed. The people, once more regarded them kindly, came to their sermons and gave attentive ear to their teaching, just as they had before.

[90] During this time many kept asking the companions whether they were the ones whom St. Vincent under divine inspiration had foretold would come one day, a holy group of evangelical men filled with zeal for the faith and outstanding in every virtue. Certainly none of the

Fathers had yet read what Vincent had written. But they responded to their questioners only with a smile as though it would be dreaming to have this understood to be about themselves; they had no taste for the lofty but associated with the lowly [Rom. 12:16]. Some years later when I was living in Portugal, the bishop of Coimbra showed me the passage in Vincent, nearly persuading himself that the Society was foreshadowed in it. Would that God, the immortal one, had brought it about that we were the ones to whom this passage might seem to be pointing, but the testimony that Vincent left places such outstanding virtue in this group of evangelical men that I certainly do not know that anyone could appropriate it to himself with any kind of humility. This is what Vincent writes:

> Three points we should especially meditate on very care-fully: first, Christ crucified, made flesh, etc., second, the state of the apostles and the rank of our brothers of the past, with a desire to be like them, third, the future state of evangelical men; and you ought to meditate on these things day and night, namely, the state of very poor, sim-ple, meek, humble, lowly people who are likewise filled with burning love, thinking nothing, saying nothing, desiring nothing except Jesus Christ alone and him cruci-fied [cf. 1 Cor. 2:2], caring nothing for this world, forget-ful of self, contemplating the supernal glory of God and the blessed ones, sighing and grasping for it from the heart, and for love of him always hoping for and desiring death itself, and like St. Paul saying, "I desire to be dis-solved and to be with Christ" [Phil. 2:23].

And so on until the end of the chapter.

---

[21] St. Vincent Ferrer, in the final chapter of his *Tractatus de vita spirituali. FN* 3:118[22].

CHAPTER SEVEN: Rome and Other Cities, 1539-40

[91] Having gained a time of quiet pregnant with opportunity, the companions decided to explain to the Pontiff the kind of life they wanted to lead to the honor of God and in the service of the Apostolic See. So that what had begun well might end well they deliberated together on the best means to use to that end. So for three months,[1] if I remember correctly, having commended themselves very carefully to God, what they had earlier decided in Paris they confirmed once more, that since it was impossible to sail to Jerusalem within the prescribed time, they would commit all their energy and their whole life to procuring the salvation of their neighbors, both believers and unbelievers.[2] They add something new, however, that one is to be selected as Superior General to be in charge of the others, as it is now;[3] then that solemn vows of obedience, poverty, chastity were to be pronounced, and finally a solemn vow of special obedience to the Sovereign Pontiff and his successors.[4] Many other things besides were decided upon conducive to their endeavor and their purpose, which I will not repeat since it would take too long a time to enumerate each one of them and especially since they can be read in the first document of the Society.[5] Taught by the experience of the ongoing years, the Fathers determined other things as well, and continue to declare, which are judged necessary for the preservation and perfection of the Society's institute.

---

[1] As a matter of fact, this deliberation lasted for three months, from the middle of Lent (which began 19 February 1539) to 24 June, the feast of the birth of John the Baptist. C 1:7. *FN* 3:120[1].

[2] The text of the deliberations is found in C 1:1-7. *FN* 3:121[2].

[3] C 1:4. *De oboedientiae voto faciendo,* C 1:8. *FN* 3:121[3].

[4] *Conclusiones sex sociorum,* C 1:9. *FN* 3:121[4].

[5] The Society's "first document" is more likely the one the companions prepared for Contarini to read to Pope Paul III before the pope gave his oral approval to the Society on 3 September 1539, a document variously known as the *Prima Summa,* or the *Five Chapters* or from its opening words, *Cum ex plurium,* (C 1:14-21), or less likely it may indicate the solemn bull of confirmation, *Regimini militantis ecclesiae* of 29 September 1540.

[92] When they had established all these things they decided to talk to the Roman Pontiff about their proposition.[6] They thought they could do this properly through Gasparo Contarini, a patrician from Venice and a cardinal, born of the noble Contarini family, who was well disposed toward the companions and was a man of sound doctrine and great probity.[7] He, therefore, in the month of September 1539 explained to the Supreme Pontiff at Tivoli the kind of life the Fathers desired to establish and all the other things that I have spoken of above, adding as well that the companions desired and fervently sought that he would open a way for others who also would like to commit themselves to this kind of life through the grace of God lest after he approved this way of life for them, it would die with them, and that they humbly and suppliantly requested that this religious order of clerks regular should be called the Society of Jesus. The Pontiff listened to all this very carefully, made the sign of the cross with great love in imparting his blessing and replied, "We bless it; we praise it; we approve it." He showed in other words as well how special the Fathers were to him, how acceptable the way of life to which they had decided to give and consecrate themselves completely.

[93] From that time on the Pontiff began to use the help of the Fathers in very important works of piety. Afterwards he sent six of them to various cities and places in Italy, namely, Faber and Laínez with the Cardinal of the Holy Angels[8] to Parma and Piacenza, Jay to Brescia, Nicolás Bobadilla to Calabria, Paschase and Simão to Siena. And although they undertook these works zealously and fruitfully, as is already clear from what others have written, I know how difficult it was and how long it took for those Fathers who went to Siena to complete their task with divine help. They had come to this city because of the prayers addressed to the Pontiff by the archbishop[9] and Ambrosio Catarino[10] and the intervention of other highly placed men,[11] for the

---

[6] The English words "proposal" and "proposition" are somewhat tentative; *propositum* in Latin indicates what they have determined to do; of course, they still needed the Pope's permission to implement the decision they had reached.

[7] Contarini died in 1542 after working hard for the confirmation of the Society. *FN* 3:122[4a].

[8] Ennio Filonardi. *FN* 3:122[5a].

[9] Francesco Bandini, archbishop of Siena. He wrote favorably of Broët. See *EB* 201-204. *FN* 3:123[7].

[10] Lancilotto de' Politi, O.P., called Ambrosio Catarino (1484-1553). *FN* 3:123[8].

[11] Among them was Lattanzio Tolomei, the vicar of the archbishop of Siena and a friend of Ignatius. *FN* 3:123[9].

avowed purpose that a certain convent[12] of holy nuns might be liberated a bit from a rather lax way of living and might be led to a more austere way of living. It was astonishing how difficult this task was made to look to them by the archbishop of the city and by Catarino, the brother of the nuns' superior, how often it had been undertaken and attempted by these important men. Nevertheless finally, with divine help, with great profit to those virgins, with peace and joy, the task was accomplished so that one could not possibly hope for a happier outcome. The Fathers preached to the nuns, heard their confessions, confirmed in the life they had undertaken their wavering and uncommitted hearts, and improved their education in matters divine.

[94] The work of the Fathers in Siena was not limited to this convent, but extended to whatever would be fruitful for people. With special zeal they tried to move to piety and virtue the nobles and all the young people who were attending school there, in whom there is much hope. For this reason one of them began to explain one of the epistles of St. Paul so that with this as bait he might more easily captivate the minds of the best youths hungry for anything new.[13] This plan turned out so well that in a very short time the talented and respected young people caught on fire. For they began, by frequent confession, to wash away the sins they had committed, and to nourish themselves much more frequently on the food of the most holy Eucharist. They eagerly visited the hospitals, were present to the poor little beggars day and night, made their beds, cleansed the sores of the sick, and freely performed the vilest tasks. They consoled the sick, comforted the miserable, the downcast spirits of those who were dying they lifted up to faith and hope and strengthened them in their faith in Christ. It happened one time that in the last struggle for some poor man's life, they were set on fire with incredible zeal for his spiritual health. For when they were present to him in his final conflict and kept reminding the dying man of the rewards of eternal happiness, although words failed him and he spoke rather brokenly, he said this one thing, "Prove that the soul is immortal." When he said this they vigorously raised up the dejected, yes despairing, soul of this man to the hope of eternal happiness. Although they had this fervor, some were aroused to improve their

---

[12] The Benedictine monastery of Sts. Prosper and Agnes. Paschase Broët had the task of reforming it. *EB* 201-203. *FN* 3:124[10].

[13] Simão Rodrigues. *FN* 3:124[10].

hearts with greater zeal in private and wanted to cleanse their consciences by means of a general confession and to spend time in spiritual exercises by themselves.

[95] So that they could pray more quietly and be more removed from
the noise and movement of people and society, he rented a house outside the walls. Its location was sufficiently suitable and it enjoyed
many other advantages where they might more conveniently engage
in pious meditations.[14] Father kept coming here every day from the
city, and he began to instruct people very fruitfully in spiritual matters. But now a rumor arises and begins to spread that some young
people are being held outside the walls cut off from normal human
intercourse. Suddenly a great rush is made on the place to see what is
going on. Meanwhile it suddenly comes to Father's mind, when sus-
pecting nothing, that he should go to the youths, and send them away
from the house, and he had no rest of mind until he gathered them
together and sent each one home. He had hardly done this when no
small portion of the populace of Siena is at hand, greatly stirred up by
the parents and acquaintances of the young men so that they might
extract the young men detained there and, if need be, demolish the
house. But when they carefully search the house and find absolutely
no one there, they return to the city baffled.

[96] Among those whom Father formed in spiritual exercises in that
later house was a priest well known throughout the city for his charming manners and witty humor and extraordinarily happy banter. He
was a genius at putting together comedies and funny tales and pre-
senting them to the public. He often went to the theater and, being a
talented mimic, he was always imitating the words and actions and
scurrilous gestures of comedians (several in the same scene) to an
excessive degree and with theatrical licentiousness. When he finally
came to regret profoundly the way he had been acting, he quite decided to change his way of living and he figured out a way in which he
could make up to the public whom he had ill served, if you look at the
example of a profligate life. So he goes to one of the Fathers and
explains to him that he wishes to manifest his repentance in one of the
better known churches of the city, and it seems to him that he could do

---

[14] It seems that this house should be called the first "retreat house," even though
it was not permanent. I. Iparraguirre, *Historia de los Ejercicios* 1:143-344. *FN* 3:125[12].

this if he put a rope around his neck and earnestly begged pardon from everyone when there was a big crowd in the church. Father first asks the man to go to the Vicar,[15] and if he gives permission, to go ahead and do it. The Vicar agreed, praised the man's plan, and gladly gave permission for him to carry it out. Happy and joyful, the priest returns to Father, and tells him the vicar's decision. Father further advises the man to consult a religious priest, a Franciscan who was a preacher in the city.[16] If he approves the action, he says, after he gives his sermon he can tell the people before they leave to wait a little longer, then you go up into the pulpit and with as much sorrow as you can implore their forgiveness. I can hardly explain here how much weeping there was in that crowd when they saw and heard this former clown, completely changed in appearance, asking for pardon in words filled with sorrow and tears. The action was a great example for everyone, and a marvel to the whole city. Afterwards he begged and pleaded to be admitted into the Society, but when that was not granted he joined the group of Franciscan Fathers (commonly called Capuchins) where he passed his whole life in great religious fervor. And I was told some years later when I came to Siena that he had gone to his rest after an edifying life of constant virtue.

[97] Those good young men who embraced goodness zealously also later gave signs of their ardor. For some of those in Siena, without consulting their parents and without their knowledge, set out for Rome to join the Fathers' company, but they were intercepted and called back by their parents right in the middle of the journey. They tried again to flee a bit more cautiously and finally made it to Rome where some were admitted into the Society.[17]

[98] Perhaps by reason of the strenuous work the two Fathers carried on in Siena to an immoderate degree, one of them broke down and became so sick that he was at death's door and was compelled to leave his companion and return to Rome.[18] There he found four others who had remained in the City who were no less hard at work.[19] They were

---

[15] Francesco Cosci. *FN* 3:126[13].

[16] Identity unknown. *FN* 3:126[14].

[17] We do not know their names, whereas we do know the names of others who entered the Society in these early days. It could be that these young men from Siena spent only a short time in the Society. *FN* 3:127[15].

[18] Simão Rodrigues, whom Ignatius called to Rome. *EM* 1:41. *FN* 3:127[16].

[19] These were Ignatius, Xavier, Codure, and Salmerón. *FN* 3:12[17].

performing various works of charity in various localities not long after that great work of charity they carried on for the poor when the prices were so high, that we mentioned above.[20]

[99] Thus far regarding what happened in Siena. I would go no farther on the same subject except for one incredible and unheard of change of heart that took place a little before the Fathers' arrival in that city. Not many miles from Siena there was a sacred shrine under the jurisdiction of Malta in which it was suddenly reported over and over again that very many remarkable miracles were being wrought there by God. For the sake of gain a huckster and some other greedy people get a rumor started, and so the shrine enjoys a large gathering of people every day. Not just ignorant and uneducated people flow in there but every kind of person of whatever rank and sex and age comes there. The surrounding fields overflow with the crowds of those arriving. In full voice they all repeatedly proclaim the miracles, and, as though out of their minds, they insanely recount the miracles again and again with loud cries. Men and women spend the night here and there without separation of the sexes. So now, what came of this great religious stir? Many who went into the chapel, where they found a little quiet from all the shouting, suddenly left the church as though they were mad, proclaiming miracles again in a loud voice. They would eagerly race in a mad rush to a certain stone, would freely throw themselves prostrate upon it, and suddenly would be snatched up by the devil and become possessed. Other pious but ignorant little ladies from Siena, who were not able to come to the shrine, kept asking eagerly how far it was from the city to this shrine. When they found out they began to designate a spot within their own private homes, which they would walk around in a circle until they had covered that distance. When they had finally done this then suddenly, as though they were mad, they also started proclaiming miracle after miracle time and again with the same outcries, and they ran around looking for a certain stone where they would also throw themselves prostrate and likewise were immediately possessed by that filthy demon. The Fathers saw many of these same women; indeed they freed not a few of them from this great evil through the sacred rites of the Church. The Fathers, therefore, frequently cursed these tricks of the mocking demons; indeed insofar as it was possible they dispelled in good part

---

[20] See [80]. *FN* 3:127[17].

this black deceptive cloud that the devil had evilly spread, and with divine help they brought relief to these tormented little women.

> *Commentary:* "Unclean spirits, crying with loud shrieks, came out of many who were possessed" (Acts 8:7), in the work that Philip the deacon did in Samaria.

[100] We have mentioned the cities in Italy to which the first Fathers were sent by the Sovereign Pontiff after the oral approbation of the Society and before they obtained the letter of confirmation. In the course of the year, also at the command of the Pontiff, they were sent outside Italy to various kingdoms and provinces of the world. I mention Germany, Poland, Ireland, France, Spain and India of the rising sun. But let us return to the confirmation lest we digress a little too freely.

[101] The Fathers accomplished a great deal of work while they were anxiously waiting for the document of confirmation. For those cardinals whom the Pontiff wanted to consider the matter with prudent care ahead of time were opposing it. Among the rest one especially resisted, Bartholomew Cardinal Guidiccioni, a truly holy man and an expert in canon law. Perhaps considering that some families of religious had grown cold and lapsed a great deal from the first fervor, discipline, and perfection of their institute, he was of the opinion that all the religious orders in God's Church should be reduced to four, and it was said that he had written a book on the subject.[21] He, therefore, was so far from saying that the Society should be confirmed that he could not be persuaded, in any way or by any argument or by anything anyone said, at least to read the written formula of the institute of the Society. The Fathers therefore run to God, pour out prayers to him unremittingly to change the cardinal's mind, and arrange for three thousand Masses to be offered to God for this intention. Suddenly he changes his mind and indicates that he would like to see and come to understand the institute of the Society. When he grasped what it was all about, he approved it to such an extent as to go to the opposite extreme, asserting that this one institute should be embraced by all the other religious men. Nevertheless, seeing no way out, he said the

---

[21] In *De concilio universali* and *De Ecclesia et reformatione ministrorum* Guidiccioni fought hard for the observance of the prohibition against new orders decreed by Lateran Council IV [1215] and the Council of Lyons [1245]. *FN* 3:130[19].

Society should not be confirmed so as not to reveal the vast multitude of religious orders existing in the Church. Finally he commended the institute of the Society very highly to the Sovereign Pontiff in a remarkable way, nonetheless adding that he could in no way approve the vast variety of religious orders.

[102] While all this is going on and there is resistance to the Society's confirmation, a year goes by,[22] and at the same time Cardinal Guidiccioni completed his span of life on earth, and departed from this life.[23] After some days the written confirmation of the Society was kindly granted by the Pontiff on 27 September 1540, as is clear in the first document of confirmation. But since the matter had been struggled over for a long time and there had been so many controversies and disputes in untying this knot, in this confirmation the Pontiff cautiously provided that the number of professed Fathers would not exceed sixty. But a little later, in view of the Society's successes, the Pontiff gave broad power to receive all those who, called by God, wanted to add their names to this institute.[24] The Supreme Pontiff was so inclined in our favor, was so good to us that even when he was about to breathe his last he bestowed singular privileges and indulgences on the Society, as can be seen in the documents.[25] For this deed of his and for many other deeds he performed that we know about, may our great and compassionate God compensate him out of his great kindness with the eternal gift of happiness.

[103] In the meantime, while these things were going on in Rome toward the promotion of the nascent Society, a certain Father who was commending the matter to God in prayer seemed to see with the utmost clarity a barren vineyard running wild in a strangulation of roots and weeds, neglected, with its vines unpruned and withering away. Then he saw very clearly in another part of the vineyard, amongst those uncultivated and withering vines, one particular vine adorned with many green leaves which were very large and delightful. From it came forth very long shoots or vine branches with

[22] Paul III approved the Society orally on 3 September 1539. The Bull, *Regimini militantis ecclesiae,* was dated 27 September 1540. *FN* 3:131[21].

[23] Clearly an error. Guidiccioni died in the Roman curia on 28 August 1549. *FN* 3:131[22].

[24] The bull *Iniunctum nobis,* 18 March 1544. *FN* 3:131[23].

[25] The bull *Licet debitum,* 18 October 1549, granted the Society many privileges. Paul III died on 10 November 1549. *FN* 3:132[24].

beautiful and abundant clusters of grapes, which had nonetheless not yet reached maturity. He saw besides that those shoots with their leaves and clusters were reaching and spreading through that wilderness of weeds, which had already made great advances, and were penetrating into the midst of the other vines and almost consuming them. But now he grasped that in seeing the abandoned vineyard running wild and unpruned, he had been given an image of the state of the Church at the time. Through the vine, however, and its branches loaded with clusters of immature grapes in that uncultivated and dying vineyard, he believed he was meant to see the condition of this yet recent Society. Finally, through the exceedingly long shoots of that vine which were taking possession of the weeds and the vineyard in that untended spot, there came to his mind the image of the Society spreading throughout the world.

[104] The same Father, again when he was at prayer, saw clearly and sharply a very beautiful tree, fairly tall, its well shaped trunk like a rounded and beautifully wrought column. The top part, moreover, formed a circle with green branches in abundance and all its parts elegantly arranged into a ring. Now whatever that tree might be, it occurs to him as he ponders, that it is a pyre, and then freely reflecting on "pyre," he kept repeating: pyre, Peter, petra. When Father concluded, "Certainly the Church is designated by this tree," then he suddenly saw a vine near the trunk of this tree, newly planted and slender, rather long, which wound around the whole trunk of the tree and began creeping ever higher, and he sensed immediately that this new vine signified the Society which first sprouted in the field of the Church and was joined to it clinging closely, and this union that Father pondered at length within himself as a marvelous and mysterious reality.

[105] Thus far I have, therefore, written in a summary manner about the beginning and origin of the Society, about the pilgrimages and different stopping places, and through everything divine wisdom guided them from the time they set out from Paris until the Society's confirmation in Rome. As for the growth of the Society that happened after these events, since they are better known, it is better that others write about them. This alone I will add at the end, it was not my intent to talk expressly about anyone apart from the rest but to tell only in a general way what was relevant to the origin and first growth of the

Society, unless by chance it seemed that certain personal matters that took place during that time ought to be included here and there. In these matters, as well as in others, if I have acted less prudently and circumspectly, it will be up to your singular prudence, most beloved Father, to expose and correct my errors wisely and enjoin an appropriate penance upon me for them. For the rest, may he be exalted in all things from whom all good comes and who works all in all.

Given at Lisbon, 25 July 1577
Your Reverence's subject and servant,

Simão.[26]

> *Commentary:* Simon's final thoughts reveal a man of optimism and enthusiasm. He is still "a man of desires," a happy man, even though at one time he was a troubled man. Lured by the attraction of the hermit life, he sought seclusion for a brief period, but in time returned to the full life of the Society. Interested in all its activities, he remained an enthusiastic and loyal Jesuit to the end of his days.
>
> In this story the Society owes him much. Writers like Schurhammer, who tell the story of the companions' pilgrimage from Paris to Venice to Loreto to Rome and back to Venice and the return to Rome, draw their facts from Rodrigues, but say little or nothing of the story's meaning, or of the chivalric spirit that shaped the companions' love and service of God. They use his stories but forget the document as a whole. They draw from Rodrigues the way creators of Gospel "Harmonies" used to draw from the Gospels: they recounted the facts narrated but neglected the personal theology that shaped each evangelist's message. The integrity of Rodrigues's work deserves respect and careful analysis.
>
> The document Simão has left us is an eye-witness account of the founding and confirmation of the Society of Jesus: a story of decisions made and not fulfilled yet soon transformed into a

---

[26] Rodrigues wrote in his own hand from the words "Given at Lisbon" to the word "Simão" and added his sign to his name. *FN* 3:134[25].

reality far beyond the dreams and desires of those who made the decisions, and of the decision that confirmed the transformation. It is a case study in the art of making a choice or "election," the term Ignatius uses in the *Spiritual Exercises*, #18 and #135-139.

One of the lessons of this document is that every discernment is open to further discernment, and in the process God may transform it into something not imagined by the discerner. The Society is always changing, since the needs of the Church and the world are always changing. That is why Ignatius was always fine-tuning the Constitutions to meet the needs of the times. What is more, as the group continues, the experiences repeat themselves in new ways. As the group expands, the group experiences of the past become the experiences of the expanded group. The story God writes in the Society today is the continuation of the story that Simon tells.

Just as Luke ended Acts with Paul waiting in Rome, welcoming "all who came to him, proclaiming the kingdom of God and teaching about the Lord Jesus Christ with all boldness and without hindrance" (Acts 28:30-31), so Simão ends his story by picturing the Society in Rome waiting expectantly for that which God is going to do in the Church, bringing us forward to the present moment where we, too, await what God is going to do in us.

When Rodrigues wrote to Father Mercurian, the Society had increased five hundredfold. The changes that had taken place in the Society in the forty years between the companions' departure from Paris and Simão's writing of the event, like the establishment of schools, were radical indeed, not unlike the changes in the Society in the forty years since Vatican II, with our contemporary emphasis on the preferential option for the poor, working with refugees of many nations, partnership with laity and others in the transformation of many of our works, and the establishment of new apostolates in spite of the diminution of manpower.

By telling his story, Rodrigues not only supplies for those of the new millennium the motives that drove the first companions, revealing the way God worked in their lives, he manages to build into his narrative a summary of the way they lived which resulted in the creation of the *Formula of the Institute* and the *Constitutions*. He shows how their daily lives reflected the *Spiritual Exercises*, including their response to the Rules for Thinking, Judging, and Feeling with [and in] the Church (much needed in his day—and in ours) and to controversial situations that troubled them and made them reflect. He does not hesitate to confront the challenge of chastity, the attraction to the solitude of the hermit life, the mystical encounter with Jesus in everyday life, the allurement of prestige, the temptation to pride, the penitential discipline of poverty for those who preach the Gospel, nor does he shrink from contests with lice and contagion and nakedness and repulsive sights and odors. He is describing, if they have the eyes to recognize it, the experiences of the 5000 Jesuits of his day, scattered in schools and churches and missions throughout the"civilized" and "uncivilized" parts of the world, and he is also describing the experiences of Jesuits throughout history, including 21st-century Jesuits engaged in a multiplicity of works concerned with "the faith that does justice." The challenges are all the same, the hopes and disappointments, the successes and failures, the support and opposition of others, the rejection and acclamation, the unattainable desires and the unexpected dreams come true, the good decisions and not-so-good decisions, the temptation to depend on one's own resources and the need at all times to depend on God in all things.

Jesus' disciples, after following him willingly into the boat, were terrified by a violent storm, and woke Jesus from sleep. "Why are you afraid, you of little faith?" he said to them, and then he calmed the sea (Mt. 8:23-26). Why, indeed, should any follower of Jesus be afraid? The Society of Jesus aspires only to walk in fidelity in the footsteps of Jesus despite blisters and blinding storms, deadening darkness, and demons of doubt. The story that our elder brother Simão has left us is not really the story of nine or ten companions, but the story of Jesus, the Lord of darkness and storm, at work in the Society that bears his name.

INDEX OF PERSONS AND PLACES

Wittenberg, 38